Zimbabwe
A Land Divided

Contents

Designed by Oxfam Design Department 708/MJ/92
Published and printed by Oxfam,
274 Banbury Road, Oxford OX2 7DZ

ISBN 0 85598 178 4   © Oxfam 1992

HARRIES/PANOS

ICANYANA

NATIONAL RAILWAYS
15
382
OF
ZIMBABWE

Robin Palmer and Isobel Birch

Victoria Falls and Zambezi Gorge

LINQUENDA HOUSE

F. W. WOOLWORTH

Baker Avenue, Harare

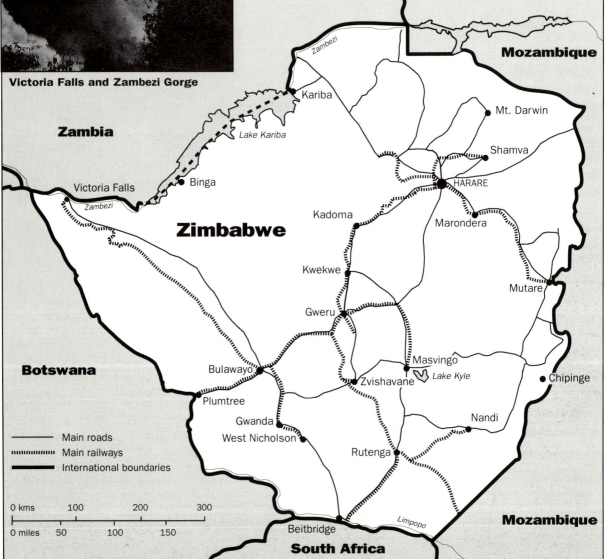

Mozambique

Zambezi

Kariba

Mt. Darwin

Shamva

Zambia

Lake Kariba

Victoria Falls

Binga

HARARE

Zambezi

Kadoma

Marondera

Zimbabwe

Kwekwe

Mutare

Gweru

Botswana

Masvingo

Lake Kyle

Chipinge

Bulawayo

Zvishavane

Plumtree

Nandi

Gwanda

West Nicholson

Rutenga

Beitbridge

Limpopo

Mozambique

South Africa

	Main roads
	Main railways
	International boundaries

0 kms   100   200   300

0 miles   50   100   150

Introduction

Zimbabwe is a land divided:

by geography – between high and low-lying areas

by climate – between regions of high rainfall and drought-prone areas

by race – between black and white

by class – between rich and poor

by ethnic differences – between Shona and Ndebele

by gender – between women and men

by agriculture – between commercial and peasant farmers

by law and history – between white-owned and black-owned land

by culture – between Zimbabwean and Western music, dance and art.

But it is also a land united by a people wanting to overcome these divisions, to break with the huge inequalities of the past, and to build a country in which all will have equal opportunities to build a better life. This book is about that past, about recent and present struggles, and about people's hopes for the future.

BRIAN BEARDWOOD/OXFAM

Village primary school, Insuza Resettlement Area

3

Spirit of the Mountain, 1990, by Sylvester Mubayi (b. 1942, a former tobacco grader, now world-famous for his sculptures, which are inspired by traditional beliefs in spiritual and supernatural forces)

Great Zimbabwe

THE COUNTRY that is known today as Zimbabwe has evolved over many centuries. A thousand years ago it had already developed its own sophisticated culture. Today it is recovering its identity after a century of exploitation, liberation struggles, and civil war.

The indigenous people of Zimbabwe who are now called Shona were mostly farmers, growing millet and sorghum in a harsh environment. On average, one year in every five brought drought. Agriculture offered people no absolute security. So, if they could, farmers tried to diversify by keeping cattle, sheep and goats, by hunting or fishing, by mining gold, by making iron or salt, or by foraging. Local communities traded with each other, exchanging their surplus goods. By the seventh century AD, the Zimbabwean plateau was linked by merchants to the great trading network of the Indian Ocean. Gold, ivory, copper, and iron were mined and exported, in return for Persian pottery, Chinese porcelain, Indian glass-ware and cloth, and commercial beads from many places. Through such trade, rulers accumulated wealth, created large states (some of which survived for two centuries), and organised the building of stone-walled towns. The most impressive is Great Zimbabwe, in the centre of the country near Masvingo. It is thought to have held an urban population of 10,000. The site was suddenly and mysteriously abandoned around 1450, perhaps because the environment had been degraded by increasing numbers of people.

In 1840 Ndebele people, driven north from South Africa by events in Natal, established a state around Bulawayo in the west of Zimbabwe. They took Shona captives and cattle, falsely claimed to rule the whole country, and later gave their name to the provinces of North and South

KEVIN DUNION/OXFAM

Ruins of Great Zimbabwe

Matabeleland. The interaction between Shona and Ndebele, and conflict between them and the European settlers who began to arrive in the 1890s, have been dominant themes in the recent history of Zimbabwe.

Boulders in Matobo National Park

MARK DAVIES

The First Chimurenga – The War of Liberation

In 1890 Mashonaland was invaded and occupied by the British South Africa Company (founded by Cecil Rhodes, who had made a fortune in the Kimberley diamond fields in South Africa). Three years later the settlers found an excuse to attack and conquer the Ndebele state too. Frustrated in their efforts to find gold, the settlers set about stealing land and cattle in Matabeleland. In 1896, first the Ndebele and then the Shona rose up dramatically and unexpectedly against their new overlords, in what is now known as the *First Chimurenga* (War of Liberation). This was the most violent, sustained, and highly organised case of early resistance to colonial rule anywhere in Africa. It was truly a people's war, involving a wide cross-section of society. It cost the BSA Company more than £7 million to suppress (an enormous sum for the time). The settlers sustained heavy casualties: 372 killed and 129 wounded – about ten per cent of the white population. The black casualty figures will never be known, though it is certain that

KEVIN DUNION/OXFAM

A memorial to Major Allan Wilson's 'Shangani Patrol', killed in battle by the warriors of King Lobengula in the last action of the Ndebele War, 1893

thousands were killed. The uprisings were put down with appalling ferocity and indifference to human suffering. People hiding in defensive positions in caves were blown up by dynamite. Those who surrendered had to do so unconditionally. Many 'rebel' leaders, such as Nehanda and Kaguvi, were hanged. Some died in prison. Others received long prison sentences. The First Chimurenga left very deep wounds, and influenced racial attitudes for decades afterwards.

The colonial legacy

The settlers named their conquered land *Rhodesia*, after Cecil Rhodes. His private enterprise, the British South Africa Company, governed the country between 1890 and 1923; then the settlers took over and ran it until 1980. They created a profoundly unequal society, which has proved very difficult to change fundamentally since Independence in 1980.

But their colonialism took other, subtler, forms too: they sought to colonise the minds of Zimbabweans – to deny them their dignity, their culture, even their history. To them, it was inconceivable that something of the size and splendour of Great Zimbabwe could have been built by people whom they regarded as barbarous savages. They created their own myths: that it was built by the Queen of Sheba, by the Phoenicians or the Arabs, or by mysterious white men who had somehow got lost in southern Africa (a fantasy that Rider Haggard exploited in his book *King Solomon's Mines*). The racism of the settlers has left deep scars in the minds of Zimbabweans; their struggles for independence and development have in part been an affirmation of the basic humanity of this once-oppressed people.

Map: The provinces of modern Zimbabwe

Emigration advertisement, 1925

White Rhodesia

'**THE WHOLE economic system of Rhodesia, on farm as well as on mines, rests on a cheap and plentiful supply of native labour.**' (*Settler politician, 1922*)

The colony of settlers in Rhodesia aimed to ensure and perpetuate white privilege and control. They dominated access to all resources, such as land, education, health, training, the road and rail networks, and loans for farming. Inequality was enforced by the settler-controlled parliament, and reinforced by social segregation. Despite such support and an abundance of cheap black labour, it was a struggle for most whites to make a living, as the early

novels and short stories of Doris Lessing testify. But Lessing left Rhodesia in 1945, just as the tide was starting to turn.

Post-war Britain, deep in debt, could no longer afford to buy three-quarters of its tobacco from the USA, and turned instead to the colonies. Rhodesia at last enjoyed a tobacco boom, based on a guaranteed market in the United Kingdom. Sales rose from £4 million in 1945 to £30 million in 1960. The number of white settlers, mostly post-war émigrés from Britain, increased from 80,000 to 220,000 in the same period, and, to make way for them, 100,000 Zimbabweans were moved off their land into 'native reserves'.

White residential suburb, Bulawayo

PETE DAVIS/OXFAM

PLEASE DO NOT PARK IN FRONT OF THE GATE

George R.B.Smith
PEASHOLM PARK
33 HEYMAN ROAD.

'UDI' and the winds of change

By 1960, as the British Prime Minister Harold Macmillan observed, the 'winds of change' were blowing throughout Africa. African nationalists were triumphant in countries to the north of Rhodesia. Seeing this, the settlers dug their heels in. They failed to obtain independence from Britain, so in 1965 they seized it illegally when Prime Minister Ian Smith and his colleagues made their Unilateral Declaration of Independence. 'UDI' was followed by the suppression of all internal political activity. Nationalist leaders such as Joshua Nkomo, Ndabaningi Sithole, Robert Mugabe, and many others were put in detention for over a decade. The world community imposed economic sanctions against Rhodesia, but only half-heartedly. Rhodesia's white-ruled neighbours, South Africa and the Portuguese colony of Mozambique, readily broke the sanctions and ensured their failure, fearing that similar barriers might later be erected against them. Eventually many Zimbabweans decided to leave their country and take up arms against the Smith regime, believing that guerrilla warfare was the only way they were going to obtain their freedom.

CHRIS JOHNSON/OXFAM

Tobacco sales floor, Harare: the world's largest auction floor. In 1965, tobacco accounted for 73% of Zimbabwe's crop sales (compared with 36% in 1989).

Roads to freedom:
the Second Chimurenga

LIKE MANY CIVIL WARS, the guerrilla war for the liberation of Zimbabwe was marked by both heroism and brutality. Civilians usually suffer most in such conflicts, and the *Second Chimurenga* was no exception.

Thousands of men and women, young and old, left the country secretly from 1970, trained as guerrillas in Mozambique or Zambia, and came back determined to assert majority rule once and for all. Since Western nations refused to arm them, they had to look to the Eastern bloc for guns and ideology. The rhetoric of the freedom fighers called for the transformation of society. The settlers, on the other hand, fought to maintain minority rule and all the powers it conferred – from control over the country's best land to the privilege of being served first in shops. Some of them tried to present their stand as a

Curfew during the War of Independence: a soldier searches women on their return from the fields to a 'protected' village

CAMERA PRESS

Helping the guerrillas

'All our food was taken away by the authorities, who would only return us a little at a time each day, just enough for one meal. But we still had to take food out to the comrades, who got angry if we failed to do so and would say, "How do you expect us to live?"

So we would put the mealie-meal into a small packet, tie it up tight, put the little bag between our thighs and then put on two pairs of pants. Every time we went through the gate of the keep the guards would make us jump, legs apart, but we could still take the mealie-meal out in this way, for when we jumped, it was quite secure. When I reached my garden, I dug a little hole and hid the bag, and the comrades would come and collect it.

Sometimes we put bags of mealie-meal in a scotch cart and then poured manure on top and said we were going to the garden. The scotch cart was always searched, but no one ever searched deeply through the manure. Again, when we got to the garden we would hide the bags at an agreed point, so that the comrades could fetch them.

If cattle were ever killed in the keep, I bought meat, wrapped it in a clean plastic bag and then covered the bag with very dirty paper and more dirty plastic bags to make something like a football for the little boys. Later someone would pick it up and take it to the comrades.'
(The words of a woman who was forced to live in a protected village ('keep') near Mount Darwin.[2])

Salisbury 1979: the first ZANU (PF) rally to be held in Rhodesia as the liberation war drew to a close

struggle for Western Christian civilisation against barbarous Marxist hordes.

The official death toll in the war was 27,500. The real figure may have been much higher. Most were innocent civilians 'caught in the crossfire', as Rhodesian Army bulletins euphemistically put it. There were inevitably atrocities on both sides, and rural communities were often faced with impossible dilemmas. One participant in the war, the footballer Bruce Grobbelaar, who now plays in goal for Liverpool, recalls in his autobiography seeing and hearing of 'some truly awful acts used to buy villagers' silence, and none worse than the regular stunt of dragging the main chief's number-one wife to the centre of the kraal [village], hacking off her top lip and making the chief eat it or be shot dead under the threat that worse would befall the whole village if any secrets were given away.' [3]

The turning point in the war came in 1974, when military defeats for the Portuguese in their African colonies led to an army coup in Portugal. The following year the former colony of Mozambique became independent under the leadership of the Frelimo party, which agreed to open the country's long and mountainous border with Rhodesia, allowing access to Zimbabwean guerrillas. As a result the war escalated rapidly.

The Lancaster House agreement

Ian Smith was forced to make a so-called 'power-sharing' deal with some moderate black leaders in 1978, but this failed to stop the war. A constitutional conference was held at Lancaster House in London in 1979 at which a compromise settlement was reached. In March the following year, Robert Mugabe's Zimbabwe African National Union (ZANU) party was the decisive victor in the country's first election to be held under universal franchise. Zimbabwe finally won its blood-stained independence on 18 April 1980.

Some would argue that if Britain had taken a tougher line earlier with the quarter of a million settlers, much bloodshed might have been averted, the economies of neighbouring countries such as Zambia would not have been crippled, and the political map of Southern Africa might have been changed for the better far sooner than it was. The UDI years, 1965-80, were wasted ones in every sense.

11

The shadow of South Africa

WHEN ROBERT MUGABE took power in Zimbabwe in 1980 he was confronted by a crisis of expectation from blacks and a crisis of fear from whites, who had been led by a censored media to believe that he was the anti-Christ incarnate. (The *News of the World* had referred to him as 'The Black Hitler'.) He endeavoured to confront white fears by appearing on television on the evening of his electoral victory to preach the virtues of racial reconciliation. He said:

> There is no intention on our part to use our majority to victimise the minority. We will ensure there is a place for everyone in this country. We want to ensure a sense of security for both the winners and the losers. Let us deepen our sense of belonging and engender a common interest that knows no race, colour or creed. Let us truly become Zimbabweans with a single loyalty.

He also offered peaceful co-existence to South Africa: 'Let us forgive and forget, let us join hands in a new amity.'

This was profoundly disturbing to a South African government which had expected the pliable Bishop Abel Muzorewa to win the election. Indeed it had pumped large sums of money into his campaign, trying to secure an outcome favourable to its own interests. Reconciliation between blacks and whites threatened by example the very core of the apartheid system. South Africa had already been alarmed by 'Marxist' victories in Mozambique and Angola. Now, unrestrained by the Reagan and Thatcher administrations, South Africa launched an intensive campaign of so-called 'destabilisation' (more accurately, armed aggression) against its neighbours, which was to last for a decade.

A region destabilised

Angola and Mozambique bore the brunt of the campaign. Parts of southern Angola were occupied by South African armed forces, and the South African government armed and funded the opposition UNITA movement. In Mozambique, South Africa backed the brutal MNR/Renamo bandits.

Zimbabwe suffered less acutely than her neighbours. There were spy scandals, involving white members of the army, air force, and intelligence services. There were attacks on individuals, such as the assassination of the ANC representative Joe Gqabi and the bombing of the ZAPU activist Jeremy Brickhill. Direct sabotage cost Zimbabwe an estimated total of US$180 million between 1980 and 1988. And in South Africa, railway rolling stock and imports for Zimbabwe were deliberately obstructed and delayed.

Such actions, and a constant stream of disinformation from Radio South Africa and 'Radio Free Mozambique', created an atmosphere of uncertainty. The former Prime Minister Garfield Todd (once

Guarding the Beira Line: Zimbabwe spent an estimated US$3bn. between 1980 and 1988 to protect its trade routes through Mozambique

KEITH BERNSTEIN/OXFAM

imprisoned by Ian Smith), speaking in London in 1986 to members of the Royal Commonwealth Society, expressed the mood of insecurity like this:

> If you are a farmer in Africa and the sky becomes darkened by an approaching cloud of locusts, the dread that they will settle on your land and destroy it drives every other thought from your mind. If you are a responsible statesman in southern Africa, concerned with good government, with sound economic policies, with the safety and progress of your fellow countrymen, you live in fear of the menacing cloud of apartheid which affects the whole of southern Africa. We can plan and work, but we know that until the situation in South Africa has been healed, we have no security.

The threat from Mozambique

For Zimbabwe, the most dangerous destabilisation took place in Mozambique, where Renamo bandits made a point of attacking the railway lines to Beira and Maputo, with the aim of forcing Zimbabwe to use the more expensive South African ports for its exports. Ironically, it was Rhodesia which had created Renamo and used it against the Mozambican government in the 1970s, but after Zimbabwe gained its independence, Renamo was forced to move its control-centre to South Africa.

Zimbabwe responded to the crisis in Mozambique by sending in more and more of its troops; at one point they were said to number 15,000. In retaliation Renamo declared 'war' on Zimbabwe in 1986, and began attacking 'soft' civilian targets in the border province of Manicaland. Schools and clinics were hit, roads mined, and a sense of insecurity created. Over 500 civilians were killed, usually with great brutality, in order to strike fear and terror in people. Peace talks at the very end of 1990 brought a temporary ceasefire along the Beira and Limpopo (Maputo) railway corridors and reduced insecurity in Manicaland, but the search for a lasting settlement in Mozambique continues.

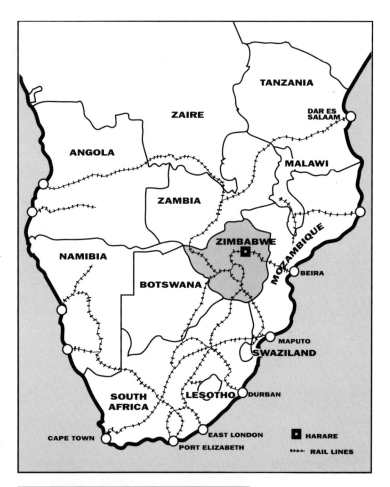

Renamo strikes inside Zimbabwe

'They came at around midnight. They robbed a shop which stored everything we needed, including food and agricultural equipment like ploughs. They took as much as they could carry from the shop. They could not even tell the food from the soap; the next morning we found that they had tried to eat several bars of soap while they were robbing the shop.

When they had finished, they set the shop alight. Later that night, they killed a woman who refused to carry their loot. They left a note to say they would be back. In the note, they said that as long as Zimbabwean soldiers were in Mozambique, they would return.'
(Village Headman, Chipinge district)

A sort of refuge:
problems on the Mozambican border

Children in Tongogara Refugee Camp: traumatised, like many others, by witnessing the murder of their parents by Renamo guerrillas

WAR IN MOZAMBIQUE has meant a steady stream of refugees entering Zimbabwe, as it has in Malawi, Tanzania, Zambia, and South Africa. In 1991, there were more than 200,000 'spontaneously settled' Mozambicans in the country, over 90,000 of whom were classified as refugees. The latter live in five camps which were originally designed to hold fewer than half that number.

But who is a refugee? The question is a complex one. Mozambicans have traditionally crossed the border to work as seasonal casual labourers on the tea and coffee estates, or daily to attend schools close to the border. At the time of Independence, Mozambicans living in the country were given the chance of obtaining Zimbabwean citizenship. Shona is spoken on both sides of the border, and Shona-speakers are prominent in the leadership of Renamo. The security issue is thus extremely sensitive and complex. Undoubtedly many people who should not have been classed as refugees have been rounded up and held in the camps, on the grounds that it is impossible to distinguish between those who support Renamo and those who do not.

Despite the close ethnic and family ties between Zimbabweans and Mozambicans in the border area, the influx of so many refugees has inevitably placed even greater burdens on local villages and government services, which were already suffering the disruption and brutality of Renamo attacks. In the words of one local doctor working in Tongogara, the largest camp: 'We don't mind treating the refugees, but the resources are limited. Our budget is to cater for the local population, but we spend 35 per cent of our working hours with Mozambican refugees, and this strains our resources. In time this may also create friction with local people, who might feel that they should be given the attention that we are giving to the refugees.'

CHRIS JOHNSON/OXFAM

Life in the camps

There are far more women than men in the camps: twice as many, according to a headcount in Tongogara in 1989. Many of the women interviewed reported that male members of their families, unhindered by the demands of childcare, had gone to look for work outside the camp, some of them as far afield as South Africa. However, despite their numbers, women are largely under-represented on the various committees which are supposed to enable refugees to share the work of running the camp.

The camps are extremely small: the largest is only 35 hectares. Environmental pressures in the area are growing as refugees use up wood for cooking and building. Local people object that trees have been cut down around sacred burial grounds. A Mozambican woman living in Mazowe River Bridge camp complained:

Life in this camp is very difficult. I travel quite a distance to go to the toilet and to fetch water. We cook for ourselves, but firewood is not available. You can see the desert which we have created around the camp. Where are we going to find firewood for our cooking? This is our biggest problem.

Map: Refugee camps (underlined)

If peace comes to Mozambique, some 'refugees' may want to remain in Zimbabwe as migrant workers, but most hope that they will be able to return home.

New arrivals at Chambuta Refugee Camp, May 1992

15

War returns to Matabeleland

BETWEEN 1982 AND 1987 an appalling conflict devastated Matabeleland, in the south-west of Zimbabwe, and almost tore the country apart.

Zimbabwe had entered Independence with a government consisting of a coalition between ZANU (the Zimbabwe African National Union, led by Robert Mugabe) and ZAPU (the Zimbabwe African People's Union, led by Joshua Nkomo). By 1980 ZANU was drawing most of its support from Shona-speaking areas, while support for ZAPU was based mainly in Ndebele areas. In 1982 hidden arms were found on farms belonging to ZAPU. Immediately, all the party's assets were seized, ZAPU ministers were dismissed from government, and key military leaders were arrested. Soldiers who had fought on the ZAPU side in the liberation war began deserting from the

Near Bulawayo: white cattle farmer armed for protection during the Matabeleland conflict

army to fight as dissidents. War returned to Matabeleland: dissidents attacked government targets, and also white commercial farmers (in order to gain coverage in the international media, white deaths being more newsworthy than black deaths). Community development activities virtually ceased.

The government responded by sending the notorious North Korean-trained 5th Brigade into Matabeleland. Gross abuses of human rights followed: thousands of civilians were killed. All signs of ZAPU activity seem to have been targets for attack. South African agents undoubtedly fanned the flames. Animosity and suspicion between Ndebele and Shona people greatly increased. Bulawayo was like a besieged city, with road blocks on every exit. Harare newspapers carried no news of Matabeleland, which seemed like a foreign country. Non-governmental organisations, both local and international, documented evidence of the atrocities and helped gradually to restrain the government.

OXFAM

Tshongokwe School, Matabeleland, damaged during the years of internal conflict

Unity – or a one-party state?

Peace was finally restored by the ZANU-ZAPU Unity Accord of December 1987. The dissidents, who had certainly fed upon popular discontent, returned home. The task of catching up on lost development opportunities began.

A symbol of peace was the announcement in 1989 that the country's second university would be located in Bulawayo. Other signs of reconciliation are the creation of the Mafela Trust, which seeks to document those from ZAPU's ranks who died during the liberation struggle, as well as moves to record the ZAPU war dead alongside those of their ZANU comrades in official war graves established throughout the country.

In 1989, ZANU and ZAPU finally merged to form one political party – the new ZANU – and ZAPU MPs joined the government side. The twenty seats which had been reserved by the British to give a sense of security to the white community had been abolished by act of Parliament

two years earlier. Most whites welcomed this, as the former Prime Minister, Ian Smith, had sat in parliament and ostentatiously spurned the policy of reconciliation, to the embarrassment of all.

During 1990, following the merger of ZANU and ZAPU, President Mugabe pushed hard for the creation of a one-party state in Zimbabwe. But the times were against him, in the democratic climate that was developing elsewhere in Africa and in eastern Europe. There was fierce resistance both from ex-ZAPU MPs and from within ZANU. Mugabe recognised the strength of this opposition and dropped the idea. Even though there are only a few opposition MPs in Parliament, Zimbabwe remains legally a multi-party state. However, this does not necessarily guarantee the survival of democratic values. The local civil rights movement, involving students, lawyers, journalists and intellectuals, campaigned vigorously throughout the 1980s, but repressive legislation introduced in 1990 threatens to undermine their efforts.

Election results: parliamentary seats held by each party, 1980-1990

Party	Party leader	1980	1985	1990
ZANU-PF	Robert Mugabe	57	64	—
PF-ZAPU	Joshua Nkomo	20	15	—
United ZANU/ZAPU	Robert Mugabe	—	—	117
UANC*	Abel Muzorewa	3	0	—
ZANU-Ndonga	Ndabaningi Sithole	0	1	1
Reserved white seats	Ian Smith	20	20	—
ZUM**	Edgar Tekere	—	—	2
		100	100	120

* United African National Council
** Zimbabwe Unity Movement

Advertisements reprinted from *The Herald,* published in Harare on 1 January 1988

The Zimbabwe Project

The Zimbabwe Project began life in London in 1978, as a European-based support group for the liberation movement. In 1981 it opened its two offices in Harare and Bulawayo, from where it now runs a varied programme of support for the co-operative movement and other development initiatives in Zimbabwe.

In its early years, the Project concentrated on helping ex-combatants after the war of independence. For social and personal reasons, it was hard for these fighters to reintegrate into peace-time society. Several of them joined together in co-operative ventures – in agriculture, business, or small industry – and turned to the Zimbabwe Project for advice and support. This work continued throughout the 1980s, and was extended to help 'dissidents' who took advantage of the government's amnesty in 1988.

Now the work of the Project has extended still further: to the wider co-operative movement in Zimbabwe, and (where possible) to 'anyone requesting help for peace and development'.

Staff provide financial, educational, and technical advice, and operate a training centre just outside Harare. They also run programmes of research, advocacy, and mediation. At the root of the Project's philosophy are values essential for the rebuilding of post-war Zimbabwean society: compassion, tolerance, and respect for the individual. Through its work, the Project puts these principles into practice, and demonstrates by example that reconciliation is possible in present-day Zimbabwe.

One enterprise that it supports is Binga Farming Co-operative, a group of 25 black farm workers who inherited Edelweiss Farm from Mr J. van Dyk, its elderly white owner. He gave it to them in gratitude for the help of his black neighbour, an ex-freedom fighter who lost his life defending the farmer against bandits in 1990. The Zimbabwe Project has lent Z$51,000 to the co-operative for the purchase of machinery, and has mediated in a dispute between the co-operative and neighbouring white farmers.

RICHARD TALLONTIRE/OXFAM

Svimuri Co-operative, Cashel: 25 members grow maize, beans, potatoes, tomatoes, broccoli, and oranges. The co-op has its own primary school and shop.

Facts and figures

Area:	390,580 sq km (UK 243,360 sq km)
Population:	9.7 million (1991 estimate)
Main ethnic groups:	Shona (77%), Ndebele (18%), others (5%)
Religion:	Traditional animist 60%, Christian 40%
Population growth rate:	3.5% per annum (estimate)
Urban population:	27% (1989)
Capital:	Harare (pop. 658,000 in 1982)
Other main towns:	Bulawayo (495,000), Chitungwiza (172,000), Gweru (79,000), Mutare (75,000), Kwekwe (48,000), Kadoma (45,000) (1982 figures)
Adult literacy:	81% of men, 67% of women (1985)
Life expectancy:	64 (1989)
Child mortality:	49 per 1,000 live births (1989) (UK: 9 per 1,000)
One doctor per:	7,400 people (1988) (UK: 1 per 650)
One hospital bed per:	443 people (1984)
Road network:	85,000 km, of which 15% tarred, 54% gravelled
Currency:	Zimbabwe dollar (Z$)=100 cents
Exchange rate in January 1991	Z$5 = £1
Exchange rate in January 1992	Z$9 = £1
Gross domestic product (GDP):	£2,605 million (1990)
GDP shares:	Manufacturing industry 26.4%, agriculture 12.9%, transport and distribution 19%, mining 8.2% (1990)
Average income:	£200 p.a. per capita (1991)
Average annual rate of inflation	11% (1980-89)
Current rate of inflation:	25% (1992)
Sources of principal exports:	Agriculture (tobacco, cotton, sugar, meat); mining (gold, nickel, asbestos); manufacturing (ferro-alloys, textiles, clothing)
Main trading partners:	UK, South Africa, Germany, USA
Foreign debt:	US$3,199 million (1990)
Debt service ratio:	24.4% (1990)

CHRIS JOHNSON/OXFAM

Agriculture and the divided land

ZIMBABWE has a single rainy season from November until March. For the rest of the year virtually no rain falls anywhere in the country. If you take the annual average, Harare gets as much rain as London. But the average is meaningless. Even during the rainy season, rainfall is unpredictable. Sometimes it doesn't come at all; at other times it falls so heavily (occasionally five inches in a single storm) that it runs away and is useless. Broadly speaking, as you move across the country from north to south or from east to west, the annual average rainfall decreases, though there are great regional and annual variations. In years when the rains fail altogether, church leaders and traditional rain makers pray for rain. In years when there is too much, crops are washed away or severely damaged. So farming in Zimbabwe has always been an extremely risky occupation, as one white farmer testified with feeling:

> In England there is no real parallel to the ruin that can be caused in Africa by a drought, or a plague of locusts, or cloud bursts. And when the main crop is a leaf crop, like tobacco, and so exceptionally susceptible, there are occasions when a year's hard work can be wiped out in twenty minutes, as I've reason to know.[4]

The great majority of black Zimbabweans are farmers. Only just over a quarter of the population live and work in the towns and cities – and nearly all of them retain economic and social links with their rural home communities. It makes good sense for them to do so, as the towns of independent Africa offer little long-term security to most of their populations.

Pre-colonial farming

In pre-colonial times, land was plentiful and population sparse, so farmers were able to move on to new land every few years. Colonial 'experts' derided this as 'shifting cultivation', but it was a very sensible adaptation to the environment. People used to grow a wide variety of crops, spreading their risks to reduce the ever-present dangers of drought and crop failure. When the Europeans colonised Zimbabwe in the 1890s, they found local peasant farmers eager to sell them food.

RICHARD TALLONTIRE/OXFAM

Zacharias Mabeteya inspects the maize crop grown by the Svishva Co-operative

This was both a way of earning cash and a means of paying the new colonial taxes. It also meant that men could avoid being taken away as forced labourers to work in the mines, where mortality rates were very high. So for the peasants, the early years of this century brought prosperity, belying later settlers' claims that blacks were incompetent farmers. But this situation did not last.

Colonial agriculture

The Europeans had come looking for gold and other minerals, but the deposits they found were disappointing. So the ruling British South Africa Company began to encourage existing and potential settlers to take up land. They were helped to do so by a package of legal and financial incentives, and by official policies designed to turn peasant farmers into migrant labourers.

The solution was simple, though it took decades to perfect. The vast majority of the best land along the high plateau, with its good rainfall and efficient communications, was given to the whites. This is the land spreading north and south of the main road and railway between Bulawayo and Harare and between Harare and Mutare. Beyond these 'White Highlands' lie the dryer middle and low-lying areas. It was into these that the

Ndebele farming in the 1860s

'Among these mountains, there are countless hills and dales, cliffs, and deep ravines, perennial fountains and meandering brooks, green fields of pasturage and gardens full of ripe maize, and various indigenous grains, ascending from the lowest valley, hill after hill, until the highest mountain top is reached.

Nearer the towns or villages, the game gives place to horned cattle and numerous flocks, and the park-like landscape is diversified by extensive fields of Indian corn and other cereals.

… The natives grow three kinds of corn, indigenous to South[ern] Africa … also ground nuts, and a species of pease, beans, a very hard melon or pumpkin, and the mealies (maize), and imfe (sweet reed) are largely planted. The fruit trees of the country are very numerous and various; some of them yielding their ripe crops, when those of others are consumed. Wild fruit is obtainable at every season of the year.

The cotton plant is grown in some parts of the Amandebele country, and the natives manufacture durable garments of it. The Amandebele grow very large quantities [of tobacco]. Indeed, I cannot remember seeing a single village around which there were no tobacco gardens.

The best and safest granary in the Amandebele land is the umlindi (hole). This is an excavation made in the ground within the kraal, with an entrance just large enough for the owner to go in and out, and widened in all directions as it descends … In these underground granaries the Amandebele corn is preserved, sometimes for many years; and in this way the natives have occasionally stored enough food to keep themselves alive during several years of scarcity.'[5]

CHRIS JOHNSON/OXFAM

Hippo Valley Estates, Chiredzi: sugar-processing plant owned by Anglo-American

majority of the black population was eventually moved. These areas were called 'native reserves', later Tribal Trust Lands, and now Communal Areas. (The population density which they now bear is over three times that of the 'white' areas.) Black farmers in these overcrowded areas could not compete with heavily subsidised white farmers. Another effect of colonialism was that peasants were obliged to grow a narrower range of crops, as maize became the staple diet of black workers and hence the main marketable crop. Grain storage systems fell into decay, because people became used to trading surpluses for cash and buying food in times of shortage.

In short, financial support, communications networks, marketing mechanisms and, crucially, political influence all loaded the dice heavily in favour of the white minority. So it was not surprising that grievances about land played such a large part in black political protest, first in the nationalism of the 1950s and 1960s, and then in the guerrilla war of the 1970s. Many people viewed the war as essentially a struggle to regain the land they had lost. They looked forward to getting it back once they had won their liberation. The year of Independence, 1980, found 6,000 white farmers, most of whom had fought tooth and nail to prevent Rhodesia becoming Zimbabwe, owning 42 per cent of the country. 700,000 black families, about 4.3 million people, were crowded into 44 per cent of the country.

Post-Independence: the prospects for peasant farmers

The first decade of Independence witnessed another peasant success story, comparable to that of the early 1900s. The peasant sector's contribution to crop sales rose dramatically from Z$12 million in 1979 (or 4.5 per cent of the total) to over Z$300 million in 1988 (or 22 per cent of all crop sales). Small farmers sold 74 per cent of the country's maize and 55 per cent of its cotton. But this apparent boom in the

TRICIA SPANNER / OXFAM

peasant economy hid huge inequalities. The bumper yields were very largely achieved in the more favoured parts of the high plateau in Mashonaland by a small minority of better-off peasants, who were able to respond to improved price incentives and to the provision of credit, advice, and research facilities, previously offered to white farmers only. These farmers were among the few who had not been expelled to more marginal lands. They represented peasants' potential, rather than the norm. The problem is that three-quarters of all peasant land lies in areas where droughts are frequent, and where even normal levels of rainfall are inadequate for intensive crop production.

Mr and Mrs L. Tembani (uncommon examples of black commercial farmers in Zimbabwe) with their tobacco crop on their recently-acquired farm near Nyazwa. Formerly a farm labourer, he was active in the War of Independence.

Land for the people:
reform and resettlement

LAND REFORM was high on the new government's agenda in 1980. It promised 'to re-establish justice and equity in the ownership of land'. But by 1990 very little had been achieved, for several reasons.

The Lancaster House constitution, in which Britain had a major hand, imposed severe constraints on the new government for a ten-year period. Land could change hands only on the basis of a 'willing seller' and a 'willing buyer', which meant that whites were free to keep their farms if they so wished. Only 'under-utilised' land required for resettlement could be compulsorily purchased, but it had to be paid for immediately at the full market price, which the owners could convert into foreign currency. These constraints were accepted by the ZANU/ZAPU coalition government only under some duress, but in return Britain agreed to fund half the costs of a resettlement programme for black farmers.

There were other factors at work. In its final years, the war had caused massive dislocation: hundreds of thousands of people had fled from the countryside to the towns or to neighbouring countries, or had been rounded up into so-called 'protected villages' by the Smith regime. Measures to control cattle disease had broken down, and people had lost a third of their livestock. All this severely disrupted peasant farmers' production, and their contribution to the country's food supplies.

The position of the white farmers

At the same time, despite the war, the white farmers were doing well. Because of the sanctions imposed on Rhodesia after UDI, agricultural exports had been hard to maintain, so the farmers had concentrated largely on the domestic market. At Independence they were contributing 90 per cent of the country's marketed food requirements. They therefore seemed crucial to Zimbabwe's immediate economic survival. Their strong position was reinforced by the advice given to the new government by Frelimo, the ruling party in Mozambique – which was to strive to retain white farmers' expertise and avoid repeating the disastrous exodus of skilled people which had taken place from Mozambique in 1975. It seemed more prudent to earn valuable foreign exchange by exporting food than to spend it on food imports. All this contributed to Robert Mugabe's policy of racial reconciliation.

Striving hard to reinforce this status quo was Zimbabwe's strongest trade union, the Commercial Farmers' Union. The CFU argues that rapid land reform would undermine the confidence of white farmers and businesses, threaten vital

Growing cabbages on a gardening project at Old Swafa, Zvishavane District, Midlands Province

BOB STORY/OXFAM

export earnings, lead to widespread unemployment, and discourage foreign investment. These arguments are not easy to brush aside in Zimbabwe's current economic situation.

Resettlement in the 1980s

So the only aspect of land reform to get off the ground in the 1980s was the resettlement programme. This involved moving black families or co-operatives, in a carefully planned way, on to land willingly sold by whites. Britain agreed to fund the operation, believing that an 'orderly and planned' programme would promote political stability. Between 1980 and mid-1989 a total of 52,000 families, some 416,000 people, were resettled on parts of the 2.7 million hectares which the government had bought for the purpose. This was far short of the national target of 162,000 families, a highly artificial figure invented in 1982. Most of the land was bought in 1981-83 and comprised whole farms in the north-east abandoned during the war. After this initial purchase, only marginal pieces of farms were offered. From 1983 the domestic budget came under great pressure, and the government felt it more politic to cut back on projected resettlement than to starve expanding health and education programmes of funds.

Even in the resettlement areas, people encountered many difficulties. They found that they had no secure title to their new land, and that they had to give up their land rights in the Communal Areas. There was also very heavy bureaucratic control, confusion among the various ministries involved, and often a lack of basic resources like farm machinery, roads, and water. In several cases the pockets of land on to which people were moved were of scarcely better quality than those they had left.

Land reform in the 1990s?

So the issue of land reform was not a priority for much of the 1980s. It was revived in 1989, in preparation for the March 1990 election and the expiry of the Lancaster House constitution in the

CHRIS JOHNSON/OXFAM

Prize bull on a co-operative cattle farm in the Midlands Province

following month. By 1991 the issue of land reform was firmly back on the national agenda. The Zimbabwean government amended the constitution to allow for the compulsory acquisition of land, with little compensation, and limited rights of appeal to the courts. This announcement provoked a crisis among white farmers, 4,000 of whom descended on Harare to question the Minister of Agriculture – the largest gathering of whites in Zimbabwe since Independence. There were protests also in banking, judicial and financial circles. An editorial in *The Times* warned that the policy 'will bring economic catastrophe' and that Britain might have to consider withholding aid for the resettlement programme. The British government's response to the 1990/91 Foreign Affairs Select Committee report on British policy towards South Africa warned that 'fresh commitments of aid in support of land resettlement must await clarification of the Zimbabwe government's policy in this area'.

Clarification came with the drafting of the Land Acquisition Bill at the end of 1991. By now, international donors to Zimbabwe's economic adjustment programme were beginning to voice concerns about the government's intentions. During a visit to Harare in February 1992, the President of the World Bank commented diplomatically: 'We think there may not have been as careful drafting as might have been desirable.' At a time of low morale in the agricultural sector, and the most devastating drought for years, the government was being warned to tread warily.

Nevertheless, a month later the Bill became law. To what extent it will resolve Zimbabwe's long and painful crisis over land, and to what extent the fears of the commercial farmers will prove justified, remains to be seen. President Mugabe's rhetorical question to Parliament hangs in the air: 'Must we stay as squatters in the land of our birth?'

Ephraim looks to the re-promised land

Gazing out at his wilting maize crop in the sandy fields of the Chiendambuya Communal Lands, 76-year-old Ephraim Nyakujara can still vividly recall the fertile farm his family used to have in the Umfusire area, his ancestral land about 60 km from his current plot, on the Harare to Mutare road. 'We could grow everything there,' he says. 'It had good soil and good water. There were wet spots where we could even grow rice. ... We had plenty of land, so that every few years we could move to new fields to let the old ones rest. Now we are all pushed together, restricted to these small fields, and we have to farm them every year. The land is tired and rocky, and the rains are bad. We farm hard, but we get bad harvests.'

The Rhodesian authorities informed his family in 1935 that they would be moved off their Umfusire farm. Nothing happened for ten years, because World War II intervened. In 1945, officials told them again they would have to move – and warned that action would be taken against those who did not.

'Transport was offered to move our things, but people were resisting,' says Ephraim. 'Then police came and burned down people's homes and harvests. Their property was destroyed. Our people were dispersed.'

The farmers were given no financial compensation. 'Hapana,' says Ephraim in Shona, with a bitter laugh. 'Not a shilling, not a penny. And we weren't given any help in settling those new lands. We were just dumped here and had to develop everything from scratch. Those were hard years.'

The resettled farmers soon discovered they could not grow many of their traditional crops on the new plots. To support his family, Ephraim went to work in hotel kitchens in Bulawayo and in Kimberley, South Africa. His seven children drifted to jobs in the cities, or to farming plots of their own. But more than 40 years later, Ephraim clings to the hope of returning to the family farm. 'I still want that land back,' he says emphatically, pointing in the south-west direction of the farm. 'I'm entitled to it. That piece of land belongs to my ancestors, and I should have it back.'

Ephraim is enthusiastic about the government's resettlement scheme, but in the meantime, he and his wife may have to move once again. The government – this time, a majority black regime – has notified him that it intends to build a Grain Marketing Board depot on their land. He doesn't know whether they will be able to stay, or whether they will be resettled and compensated. For him it is a bitter quandary.

'How can I move now?' he asks with a shrug. 'I am old, and I don't have the power to farm new fields. The younger people here will go to the resettlement areas and it will be good because they will be able to grow more. But I don't know what I'll do.'[6]

'The fields grow dust and stones': drought grips Zimbabwe

DROUGHT has always been a major threat to farmers in Zimbabwe. But, as with so much else in this divided land, it is not a threat faced equally by all. The racial division of the land has left virtually all the white farming areas within the higher-rainfall zones, while three-quarters of the black peasant areas fall within the zones of least rainfall, which are best suited either to extensive ranching or to drought-resistant crops only. The people who were forced to live there now have few options but to try growing crops for their own subsistence. It would be too risky to try to survive by selling cattle alone.

The south and west of the country had been grappling with the effects of drought throughout much of the 1980s, but by 1992 the problem had spread across the country (and indeed, across the whole of southern Africa) to become one of the worst droughts in living memory. By January 1992, Bulawayo was reported to have had only 15 weeks of drinking water left; by March 1992 Lake Kyle, Zimbabwe's second largest lake, was down to 0.8 per cent of its capacity, and the government had declared a state of national emergency. Stocks of maize had almost run out, and the government made plans to import two million tonnes to avert starvation. Thousands of cattle had already died from lack of water and grass, or had been slaughtered for lack of feed; crops of cereals, soya beans, sugar cane, oilseeds, and cotton withered in the relentless sun. Ironically, farmers predicted a record crop of tobacco – almost the only crop to escape the drought unscathed.

It is possible to travel from an area of desperate drought and hardship to discover, not very far away, an immaculate rugby pitch kept green and soft by an array of sprinklers. Even more ironic is the fact that people are seriously at risk from hunger in the areas of drought, while in good years Zimbabwe can export thousands of tonnes of food to its neighbours. Most white farmers, shored up by decades of financial support, use irrigation extensively, so that – until recently – drought was not a word in their vocabulary.

For decades farmers and planners have dreamt of tapping the waters of great rivers, such as the Zambezi, the Limpopo, and the Sabi, to 'make the desert bloom'. The dreams persist, but the costs have always been prohibitive. A much more practical approach is taken by local communities, trying to improve their situation by sinking dams and wells, by adopting small-scale irrigation projects, or by reviving traditional grain-storage techniques. As with so many other development initiatives, success is much more likely when communities themselves take charge, rather than when outside experts tell them what to do.

Dried-up bed of the Matorakurku River ('The One That Washes Chickens Away')

Beating the drought

'I was born in 1927 and have known the Midlands of Zimbabwe all my life. It's always been a dry area – very dry – but the drought was never, I think, as bad as it is now.

I first became interested in how to farm this land better when I lost my job on the railways in 1964. They threw me out because I was interested in trade unions and wouldn't obey them when they said I had to stop talking about politics. First I was restricted, then they sacked me.

I was married in 1950 and had a growing family to raise. For my family to survive, I had to learn to be a better farmer. I became very interested in how soil and water can be used badly and wasted – and in how they can be used well. I experimented with many things: with field terraces and pit reservoirs, and with ways of harnessing the water as it ran off the smooth granite rocks. And slowly I did become a better farmer! I made the first well around here, and the first improved toilet.

In 1981 I was asked to lead a well-digging programme, and in 1987 I started the Zvishavane Water Project. The drought had begun to get worse since 1985, and I wanted to do more to help people become more self-reliant. The project has grown a lot since then: we are now 12 people, mostly working out in the field, with funds from several agencies. Our main projects are now dams, tanks for rainwater collection from roofs, fishponds, and gardens. We are going to schools to set up the roof collection systems. This will help to spread the message: the children see how it works, and go home and tell their parents. And then they might want to set up a tank too. We also want to encourage people to plant indigenous trees, because they do so much to save soil and water.'
(Zephaniah Phiri, the founder and Coordinator of Zvishavane Water Project, interviewed in December 1991)

'The project has grown over time, but we are careful not to grow too fast. We provide advice, instruction and the necessary materials, and the communities themselves give the labour. At one of the dams we are building now, there are 200 people working hard to get it ready for the rains.

… One of the most exciting things about this project is that it can help to break the vicious circle of poverty. The message spreads when people see that something can work – it can help them to grow more food or get more water. When a dam is complete, you can watch it fill with water over time and know that this is really helping. It's satisfying to know that we have made a contribution like that.'
(Charles Hungwe, administrator of the Zvishavane Water Project, interviewed in December 1991)

Community labour on a dam in Masvingo Province, organised by the Zvishavane Water Project

Zephaniah Phiri (right) at the Muche-kwachekwa Dam

Taming the environment – or working with it?

ENVIRONMENTAL ISSUES, like so many other things in Zimbabwe, have always been closely linked to politics and to race. In the colonial days the white settlers believed almost as an article of faith that blacks were feckless people who didn't care for or even understand the environment and, given half a chance, were liable to ruin it. By contrast, the settlers saw themselves as rational, scientific beings seeking to impose a neat colonial order on an environment which needed to be 'tamed'. This belief was further entrenched when colonialist land policies pushed blacks into small 'reserves' in which the soil rapidly became eroded. The country's first Natural Resources Act was passed in 1941. It quite consciously sought to protect the environment from the local people.

Game conservation

Such beliefs also lay behind colonial notions of hunting and game preservation. Vast game parks were created in Zimbabwe, as in other colonies, from which local people were evicted, or in which they were prevented from hunting – while the lions, elephants, hippo and other wild animals were slaughtered by white big-game hunters. Later the game parks were turned into tourist resorts, and slaughtering was replaced by conservation.

The conflict of interest between people and animals is almost as old as Africa itself. Now it is fought between Zimbabwean game rangers and well-armed poachers, many coming in from Zambia, who are attracted by high prices for ivory and rhino horn in the Middle East and elsewhere. Many rangers have been killed. Zimbabwe has been criticised for its attitude towards the protection of endangered species. The government argues that unlike East Africa, where most of the game has already been killed off, Zimbabwe has managed to preserve its wildlife: so a policy of controlled culling, which prevents overpopulation and also provides financial incentives to local people to care for the wildlife, is a better answer. In line with this policy, many white farmers have moved into game ranching: the 'farming' of wildlife on their land for profit. This development may lead to a wider distribution of wildlife, but it has been strongly criticised because land that could produce food crops is being used to run game.

The urban environment

By Western standards the towns and cities of Zimbabwe are remarkably clean and well cared for. This is helped considerably by the government's ban on canned beer and soft drinks. The deposit charged on

Black rhinos in the Matobo National Park

MARK DAVIES

29

KATHLEEN BLADES/OXFAM

Litter-free square in central Harare

bottles of beer and Coke ensures that someone will return them. Indeed, in many places it is not possible to buy a drink unless you supply an empty bottle. The packaging of goods in shops is not so elaborate as in Western supermarkets, and this too helps to reduce waste.

A conflict of interests

Many colonial notions survive and flourish in independent Zimbabwe. There is still a strong tendency in official circles to undervalue the skills and environmental knowledge of local peasant farmers, and to assume that planners

always know best, as, for example, in the matter of land resettlement. There is also a contradiction between the needs of rural black farmers and the interests of the mainly white and urban conservation lobby, which runs a sophisticated media campaign in support of its aims, filling Harare's supermarkets with promotional T-shirts.

A different approach to conservation is taken by the many local communities and non-governmental organisations which are deeply concerned with environmental issues like the management of land and water resources, or with growing industrial pollution. Some are pioneers in experiments to develop intermediate technology appropriate to the local environment.

A major present threat to the environment concerns the Zambezi Valley in the north. Here prospectors are searching for oil. If they find it, there will inevitably be fundamental change and damage to a unique and vulnerable environment. The rapid increase in oil prices which accompanied the Gulf War illustrates the dilemmas for a country like Zimbabwe. If oil is found, Zimbabwe's economy may be strengthened, but at devastating cost to the environment.

Zimbabweans do not appreciate lectures from British environmentalists who ignore the fact that Britain's own economic and industrial growth was achieved at a similar cost. They also point out that while in Western countries 'the green issue' is in danger of becoming the exclusive concern of the urban educated middle classes, for the rural poor in Zimbabwe, in a difficult and often hostile environment, the issue is absolutely fundamental to their lives.

BRIAN BEARDWOOD/OXFAM

Appropriate technology in action: improvised bellows at Hlekweni Rural Service Centre

Changing roles for women

A commonplace view, widely held in the West, is that African women do all the work, while men loaf around chatting and drinking. Like much else in modern Zimbabwe, this generalisation can be understood only in the context of the colonial past, which fundamentally altered working and social relationships between men and women.

In pre-colonial times there was no serious conflict of roles. Women had considerable power in the domestic sphere, while men exercised more formal authority in the public domain; but the two were regarded as equally important. The woman's authority and status within her family group gave her the right to claim its protection if she was badly treated, or divorced or widowed. She gained prestige through the number of children and grandchildren she had. Grandmothers enjoyed a special authority.

Women did most of the farming, while men hunted and herded cattle. Women were also involved in clearing land and harvesting, usually with the help of relatives. They shared supplies of food, which reinforced kinship bonds, especially when the food was kept for special feasts and celebrations. Women had sole control over the distribution of all food in the home. In addition to family plots, women usually had small gardens of their own, and could do what they liked with the food they grew on them. In the 1890s, they grew beans and groundnuts on their own plots, and sold them to the new settlers.

The impact of colonisation

The Victorian colonisers of Zimbabwe believed firmly that a woman's place was in the home, and their laws attempted to impose this belief on the local people. But it was in the economic sphere that they had most impact. The loss of land, eviction to increasingly overcrowded reserves, restrictions on hunting and cattle ownership, and – above all – the migrant labour system combined to make women's position less secure and more burdensome than it had previously been.

Male migrant workers were away from home for months on end, sometimes returning only once a year; in extreme cases some even stayed away for several years. So gradually women had to take on

Mrs Sara Dube and her son Praise God, preparing supper for her husband, his mother, their daughter, and six nieces and nephews on their homestead in the Insuza Resettlement Scheme

BRIAN BEARDWOOD/OXFAM

sole responsibility for all domestic economic activities, while men earned wages and sent back to the villages as much or as little as they chose. Those men who stayed on the land tended to grow cash crops, rather than food for their families' subsistence. Agricultural support services and very limited amounts of credit were offered, but only to men.

Eventually men came to monopolise modern techniques, and so the division of labour began to change. Men's crops were not for home consumption, but for sale. For the first time, food crops became a source of individual gain, rather than nourishment for the whole family. In effect, women and men farmed as separate individuals, using different methods, and achieving very different levels of production. As women's productivity decreased, this led to greater hardship, a loss of prestige, and an ever-increasing workload.

Restrictions on the ownership of cattle meant that cash, instead of cows, was used more and more commonly in marriage transactions. This reduced the status of a woman, removed her right to exercise authority within her family (since she no longer brought cattle into it), and hence removed the family's responsibility for her in cases of bad treatment, divorce or widowhood. So women faced both economic and social insecurity. As land holdings fragmented, so too did the large family units once presided over by grandmothers. When children went to school, their labour was often lost to their mothers. The society and the economy became more individualistic, something which was encouraged by the colonial state and church. So colonialism profoundly affected both women and men, but in very different ways.

Liberation at last?

The thousands of women who became actively involved in the war of liberation, as guerrilla fighters, informants or carriers, hoped that Independence would mean an end to a century of oppression: for them, talk of transforming society was not simply empty rhetoric. Indeed, since Independence some major legal and social reforms have been won. The Ministry of Community Development and Women's Affairs was established in 1981, with the aim of removing the various barriers to women's full participation in national development. In 1982 the Legal Age of Majority Act gave women for the first time the status of adults. Previously they were treated as minors under the guardianship of their husbands. Three years later, the Matrimonial Causes Act allowed women to benefit from a share of the couple's property on divorce. There have been other progressive laws regulating women's employment.

Women have also actively organised themselves, both through village-based associations and through urban-centred lobbying and pressure groups. However, their success has so far been limited, for the structures which favour men against women, and the old against the young, remain largely in place. Male defenders of the status quo talk self-righteously of 'African tradition'; but social and cultural pressures often lead unsupported women, especially in the towns, to dump their babies or turn to prostitution. Every legal and political battle that women have fought since Independence has been a tough one.

Masvingo: a women's chicken-rearing project, funded by the sale of crochet work

TRICIA SPANNER/OXFAM

Jetina Mugwira's story

'My name is Jetina Mugwira and I have lived here in Chisarasara for 21 years. I moved here when I got married – it is our custom to move to the husband's home area. Before my marriage I lived in Shiku, near Zvishavane. That's where I was born in 1948, and where I went to school from the age of 12 till I was 18. I come from a family of nine, but we are only seven now. One brother was killed in the liberation war and my father, who drove trucks for the asbestos mine in Zvishavane, died last year. My mother still lives in Shiku and I like to see her when I can. But Shiku is some way from here, and transport is very difficult. I last saw her in May this year.

I have nine children. The oldest is now married with children of her own. So I am a grandmother. My second daughter is at college. The other children are all at school, except for my youngest daughters – triplets aged four and a half – who are at pre-school. My husband drives a truck for Coca-Cola in Masvingo. In 1980 I also started working – as a Village Community Worker, for which I am paid Z$70 a month. There are two hundred families in my round, and my main work is to encourage good child-care and teach about Primary Health Care – about the importance of clean homes and proper toilets. I also try to help groups to come together for projects to make money or grow food.

The main problem that I see in my work is malnutrition. This is because of the drought which has been with us for so many years. Since 1980 the rains have been bad, and each year it gets worse. The fields grow dust and stones.

Collecting water for drinking and cooking is very hard work. Three times a day we women must walk two and a half kilometres to get water, then carry heavy tins back to our homes.

I have hopes for the future. For my family I hope that the rest of my children can finish schooling. I want them to have proper education, so that they will be happy with good jobs and a good life. But I see problems. The cost of everything goes up – school fees too, and we don't earn enough to save much money. It is the same for most people here. Some of us have got together for projects to raise some money – soap making, sewing school uniforms and crocheting, cattle fattening and gardening. If we can keep these ventures going and make them stronger, maybe they will help to solve some problems. People are working hard and trying hard – but really, in this drought, without water, moving forward is very difficult.'
(Mrs Jetina Mugwira, Chisarasara, Masvingo Province, August 1991)

Masvingo: women's crochet group. The sale of bedspreads and tablecloths helps to supplement these farmers' incomes.

33

Education:
'the birthright of every Zimbabwean'

COLONIAL EDUCATION was about colonising the mind. Rhodesia never quite went to the lengths of South Africa's Bantu education system, which was designed to produce docile labourers, but the difference was perhaps more one of style than of substance. Official funds were meagre, and much education was left to the church missions. The first government secondary school for blacks was not established until 1945, and the first teacher-training college nine years later. Until 1965 only two schools in the entire country offered sixth form classes to blacks. Education was compulsory for white children, of whom 80 per cent completed secondary school. By contrast, fewer than 50 per cent of black children managed to enrol at primary school, and of these a mere one per cent reached the end of their secondary education. Apart from the University, founded in 1957, the educational system was segregated. Ten times more money was spent on each white child than on a black child.

The system was designed to produce a very small and predominantly white élite. It was a system that obviously had to change at Independence. It did, as the statistics reveal: the number of primary schools almost doubled between 1979 and 1989, and the number of secondary schools increased from 177 to 1,507. The number of children in school increased from under one million to nearly three million. In addition, the total number of university students rose from 1,506 in 1976 to 8,123 in 1989. These figures do not tell the whole story, because they exclude

School at Simukai Co-operative

the many unregistered schools, and they cannot record the human resources which made them possible and which represent a long-suppressed thirst for knowledge.

Progress since Independence ...

Immediately on Independence, the government pronounced that education was the birthright of every Zimbabwean, and it introduced free primary education. It hoped to provide a primary school within 5km and a secondary school within 11km of every child in the country. As this would demand immense resources, the government appealed to local communities and foreign donors. Under a self-help approach which proved remarkably successful, parents were encouraged to take the initiative, especially in the building of primary schools, and to provide materials, expertise and labour. Between 1986 and 1988 the government allocated 22 per cent of its budget to education; the equivalent figure in Britain for the same period was a mere 2 per cent. Racial segregation in schools ended, to be replaced by class segregation, as rich black and white parents sent their children to fee-paying private schools.

There was also an astonishing expansion, involving literally hundreds of thousands of people, in non-formal education, such as adult literacy classes, night classes, and study groups. Women in particular were keen to catch up on their years of lost education. Adult training in a wider sense was also expanded, and institutions such as Hlekweni, Silveira House, and Glen Forest offered people access to the practical skills, relevant to a rural environment, which had been denied them under colonialism.

... and problems

There is, inevitably, a negative side. Greater educational aspirations have also meant stretched resources, overworked and under-qualified teachers, far too many students paying to sit exams that

they have no hope of passing and, tragically, at the end of this hard-won schooling, very severe rates of unemployment. In part the problem is one of content, in part one of attitude. Despite various alternative experiments, the system remains much as it was, fundamentally élitist and geared towards academic skills that are of little use either on the land or on the urban job market. As elsewhere in Africa, attempts to restructure the syllabus to make it more relevant to society's real needs have been fiercely resisted. With an academic education come academic attitudes, and hostility towards other forms of skill and knowledge.

The government had to offer education to the people, given the long neglect of the colonial years – and the people have responded with enthusiasm. To provide them with employment is altogether more difficult. Growing numbers of trained but unemployed secondary school leavers and even graduates represent a potential threat to the stability of Zimbabwean society, as the government knows all too well.

Classroom at Hlekweni Rural Service Centre

BRIAN BEARDWOOD/OXFAM

**Carpentry class at
Hlekweni Rural
Service Centre**

Hlekweni, the place of laughter

*'Hlekweni was born out of struggle
and repression during the years of
UDI. It was an expression of hope
and faith in the future, while all
around was evidence of death.'* [7]

Situated just outside Bulawayo,
Hlekweni Friends Rural Service Centre
is both a working farm and a training
centre which offers practical courses
in rural technology and agriculture. The
training, for both women and men,
covers a wide variety of activities, from
carpentry to roof-thatching, from
poultry-keeping to metal-work. Some
takes place at the centre; some in
extension work in the rural
communities. Most of the courses at
the centre are for short periods of up
to a year, and are then followed up by
the centre's staff after the students
return home.

But Hlekweni is more than a training
centre: it is a community of people
committed to the ideals of its
founders. It was established in 1967
to serve the rural population of
Matabeleland, and became a haven of
multi-racial peace amid the violence
and repression of the post-UDI years.
Restrictions on travel in Matabeleland
were tightened during the 1970s,
which limited the centre's outreach
work. But it continued to demonstrate
an alternative way of life, based not on
repression and division, but on
interdependence and fellowship.

'Hlekweni' means 'the place of
laughter'. Today, despite Zimbabwe's
growing economic problems and rising
unemployment, the centre continues
to respond to the nation's needs with
cheerfulness, hope, and a simple
belief in the importance of people.

Health for all by the year 2000?

BEFORE INDEPENDENCE, the provision of health care in Zimbabwe was just as uneven as the provision of education. Health services were overwhelmingly directed towards the whites, the cities, and expensive curative medicine. Half the doctors were in private practice, almost entirely serving white patients. Meagre government services for black people were supplemented by the church missions, which provided 60 per cent of rural health services. In Bulawayo in 1976 three general hospitals served a white population of just under 70,000, while one general hospital served a black population of just over 400,000. Not surprisingly, the black population suffered from substantial childhood malnutrition, from a high infant mortality rate (caused partly by inadequate immunisation), and from low rates of life expectancy. If you were rich and white, you were likely to enjoy good health; if you were poor and black, you were not.

An integrated national health service

After Independence the government sought to transform the health services, to create an integrated national health system, and to involve people in their own health care, by training village health workers. Primary Health Care, with an emphasis on the mother and child and on preventative medicine, was adopted as national policy. Free health care was available to everyone earning less than Z$150 per month. It was hoped to provide some health-care facility within 8 kilometres of every home. To try to achieve 'health for all by the year 2000' it was necessary to ask for help from overseas donors, and this was given generously.

Great strides have been made towards bringing health care to those most in need, expanding the services, and distributing them more fairly. The numbers of medical staff have doubled at all levels. Urban-based, curative medicine no longer dominates the national health-care budget. The government has adopted a policy to restrict the import of expensive non-essential drugs, and Zimbabwe now produces over half of its own drug requirements. Traditional healers have their own recognised national association,

Rehabilitation Unit at Glenview Clinic, Harare

BRIAN BEARDWOOD/OXFAM

whose members are licensed to practise alongside the conventional services. There is far better ante-natal care for women. Cleaner water and better sanitation have been provided, often with enthusiastic help from villagers.

In statistical terms, 80 per cent of children aged between one and two years are now fully immunised against measles, TB, whooping cough, tetanus, diphtheria and polio. In 1989 the infant mortality rate was almost half what it was at Independence; life expectancy at birth rose from 45 in 1965 to 57 in 1989; and the number of rural clinics increased from 247 in 1979 to 1,062 in 1989. Zimbabwe has been praised for its progressive family-planning programme, and has the highest rate of contraceptive use in sub-Saharan Africa: 43 per cent of women currently make use of modern contraceptive methods.

None of this would have been possible without the active involvement and commitment of rural people, especially women. They are involved as village health workers and birth attendants; they provide materials and labour for the building of clinics, toilets and wells; and they have willingly attended courses in health education and care. What all this meant to people was expressed in 1990 by a woman from the north of Zimbabwe:

> Several years ago even minor illness could mean death. We had no access to clinics or doctors. The nearest hospital was several days' travel. Now we have our own clinic in the village which can deal with most problems, and if there's a serious illness, transport can be provided for more specialist care.[8]

... but many problems remain

Despite the impressive achievements of the Zimbabwean health services since Independence, equal access for all has not been attained. As in education, the barriers of race have been replaced by the barriers of social class. Zimbabwean doctors, trained at huge government expense, move rapidly into lucrative private practice. All attempts to bond them to work for the government have failed, and even provoked strikes on occasion. Another cause for concern is the health care of vulnerable refugee populations in camps in the east.

The AIDS virus is hitting Zimbabwe hard. According to the World Health Organisation there were 109 cases of AIDS per 100,000 of the population in Zimbabwe in 1991, one of the highest reported rates in Africa. The death of a white Zimbabwean doctor in Britain in 1988, and the sensational press coverage it received in the British tabloids, led the Zimbabwean government to adopt a disastrous policy of secrecy about the illness for some years. AIDS sufferers wrote desperate appeals in magazines like

Village health workers on a training course near Nkayi, Midlands Province.

CHRIS JOHNSON/OXFAM

Parade, claiming that no counselling was available. The new Minister of Health, Dr Timothy Stamps, has put an end to that. AIDS is now back on the national agenda and can be openly discussed. Official campaigns have been launched by health officials and politicians (though the role of the churches has been disappointing), and it is now estimated that 86 per cent of women have heard of AIDS.

Dr Stamps has also tackled the powerful local tobacco industry, with public warnings that smoking is bad for health. He is the first Minister of Health in the country's history to have done this, and has predictably drawn upon himself the wrath of the tobacco companies. The struggle for good health thus continues – against many obstacles.

WINNING NEW GROUND IN AIDS WAR

Sir – Much of the news about AIDS is gloomy, but your readers might be encouraged to know that people in the Mutorashanga area have taken up the challenge, and are not only changing their lifestyles, but also using condoms.

There are books on AIDS for free reading in all the stores, butcheries, garages, and even the Post Office, in addition to condoms being there too. More than 5,000 condoms are taken every month, as well as what is collected by farm-workers on as well as what is collected by farm-workers on pay-days, and a further 25,000 go out to other farms.

There is far less sexually-transmitted disease being treated on this farm by the visiting clinic than there was four years ago when the Commercial Famers' Union started this pilot scheme.

The scheme is being extended to cover as many farms as possible, and I hope that farm workers will encourage their employers to join in the scheme, and will form AIDS committees like the one we have.

In parts of Uganda, more than a third of the population are orphans. We have not got enough grandmothers for that here. The only way to kill AIDS and the fear of it is by practising prevention ... always.

– J.P. Fraser-Mackenzie, CFU AIDS co-ordinator, Lone Cow Farm, Mutorashanga.
(Letter to *Parade*, April 1990)

Zimbabwe National Traditional Healers' Association

It is estimated that up to 80 per cent of people in Zimbabwe make use of traditional medicine. Including the women who are served by traditional midwives, this figure is even higher. Traditional healers have always taken a holistic approach to their patients, addressing not only the physical symptoms, but also any social or psychological factors which may be related to the illness. Counselling plays an important part in their work.

Approximately 30,000 traditional healers are practising in Zimbabwe today, and ZINATHA, their national organisation, operates 312 branches across the country, which run workshops, meetings, and training courses. The healers are very influential in their communities, not only on questions of health, but also on cultural and social matters. In this respect, their position enables them to play a valuable role in health education.

In 1989 ZINATHA joined the government's anti-AIDS education campaign, in a concerted effort to fight the rapid spread of the disease. Some traditional family practices, such as polygamy or the 'offering' of a widow to the brother of her husband, which are liable to increase the incidence of the disease, may best be addressed with the co-operation and understanding of traditional healers, and by respecting their status in society. Despite their different approaches to health care, ZINATHA and the government are demonstrating the value of mutual respect and co-operation by working together to tackle one of Zimbabwe's most serious contemporary health issues.

The disability movement

ASURVEY in 1983 revealed that an amazing 10 per cent of the population of Zimbabwe, or about 800,000 people, suffered from some form of disability. Many people were disabled through being 'caught in the crossfire' during the armed struggle for independence, and others because immunisation programmes had broken down during the war. Poor health care in the rural areas under colonial rule was also to blame.

The new government's response was to decentralise services to the rural areas, and to involve the families of disabled people in the process of rehabilitation. Rehabilitation assistants are trained and sent out to demystify the issue, promoting more positive attitudes towards people with disabilities, so that families and communities can help the disabled to help themselves. Village workshops, theatre groups, and the mass media are all used to challenge negative thinking about disability. This is a very different approach from the standard Western practice, with its heavy reliance on institutions and professional care. The emphasis in Zimbabwe has been on integration – in communities, in schools, and in the government's own health structures. The community-based rehabilitation programme falls under the general responsibility of the Department of Maternal and Child Health, which means that rehabilitation assistants and therapists are able to work in closer co-operation with colleagues in related fields, such as immunisation, nutrition, and health education.

Even more important than official attitudes is the very active and forceful constituency of disabled people themselves. It includes organisations such as the National Council of Disabled Persons of Zimbabwe (NCDPZ), the Southern African Federation of Organisations of the Disabled (SAFOD), and the Zimbabwe Association for the Disabled. These are campaigning groups which constitute a common movement. They like to distinguish themselves from the multitude of welfare organisations which preceded them, and from which some of them broke away. Those groups tended to focus solely on the material needs of disabled people. They are still largely led by able-bodied people, who feel that something should be done to improve the position of the 'less fortunate'.

The campaigning groups have rebelled against this well-intentioned but patronising mentality. 'Disability does not mean inability' is their slogan, and they fight for recognition as they are, as full

The staff of Freedom House, headquarters of the National Council of Disabled Persons of Zimbabwe, in Bulawayo

RICHARD TALLONTIRE/OXFAM

members of society. They claim their rights, and not just privileges which others may (or may not) confer upon them. Their movement is essentially a political one, designed to change prevailing social attitudes. They want to lead themselves, to speak for themselves, and to work for their living. A major element of their struggle is organisation: locally, nationally, regionally, and internationally. Although they have such long-term objectives, they also believe that what can be done today should be done today; for example, they press for equality of employment, better access to buildings and public transport, an end to discrimination against people with disabilities, and greater economic self-reliance for their organisations. NCDPZ, for example, operates a supermarket in Bulawayo, managed and run almost entirely by people with disabilities.

In Zimbabwe the disabled people's organisations are all involved in the politics of disability. They campaign for the basic human rights of their members, and especially for the right to control their own lives, and to take part in the life of the community. They have made their mark since Independence, and are now a major social influence on government and other sectors of society.

The world is not the same any more

People like physiotherapists and occupational therapists and social workers – they think they have solutions to our problems. They don't see us as belonging to society. They think we belong to them: they keep files on us throughout our lives, and decide when I should see the doctor. But I want to decide when I see the doctor.

These professional workers resist the disability movement, because they see it as taking power and control away from themselves. Of course, in liberation you must liberate both the oppressor and the oppressed. Changing attitudes is a very difficult thing. We see SAFOD and NCDPZ as liberation movements.

Disabled people have been passive for thousands of years, and we just started organising about ten years ago. There has been a lot of energy released from disabled people. They see themselves and their issues in common with other oppressed people. The world is not the same any more.

(Joshua Malinga, Southern African Federation of the Disabled)

PETER COLERIDGE/OXFAM

The Freedom Supermarket in Emakhandeni Township, Bulawayo. Nine of the 12 staff are people with disabilities.

The economy: sold to the highest bidder?

'**S**EEK YE FIRST the political kingdom', was the advice of Kwame Nkrumah, Ghana's first president, to fellow African nationalists in the 1950s. It was disastrous advice, for the implication was that once you had political control, everything else would follow easily. So, in the 1960s, the economic sphere tended to be neglected. By the 1990s the serious economic problems facing many African countries are only too evident. Zimbabwe, which gained Independence two decades later than most other nations, provides an interesting case study.

The colonial economy

The white Rhodesian settlers built political structures to serve their own interests. They alone had an effective voice, because all but a handful of blacks were excluded from voting until 1962. Particular groups of settlers, such as the farmers, also lobbied vigorously for their own ends. The Rhodesian Parliament could pump money into white agriculture or education and deny it to black farmers

Canteen at the Coca-Cola factory, Southerton Industrial Estate, Harare

CHRIS JOHNSON/OXFAM

or teachers. (It is interesting, though, to note that some of the settler government's fiercest battles for control of the economy were against transnational corporations. Companies such as the British South Africa Company and Anglo-American (whose interests lay mostly in mining), British American Tobacco, Liebigs (canned meats), and Tate and Lyle (agricultural commodities) were strong enough to resist any proposed change that did not suit their interests.)

The settlers built profoundly unequal economic structures to match the political ones. The whole colonial economy rested in the early days on cheap black migrant labour. Whites typically were overseers of black workers on farms, mines, railways, and in industry; most disdained hard manual labour themselves.

Mining and agriculture were the original pillars of the economy, but after 1945 Rhodesia began to diversify into manufacturing and secondary industry. The UDI years and the imposition of international sanctions against Rhodesia encouraged even further diversification. At Independence the country was producing over 8,000 different items, compared to only 600 in 1965. But UDI also resulted in a prolonged lack of foreign investment in things like communications. Even now, in Harare alone, an estimated 35,000 individuals and businesses are on the waiting list for telephone lines to be connected.

Today, Zimbabwe's economy is far more diversified than that of most African countries, and it is certainly the strongest in southern Africa after South Africa. This means that it is not nearly as vulnerable as Zambia, whose economy is almost entirely dependent on copper. But white-owned companies had almost total control of the economy in 1980, and after a decade of independence they still retain their dominance of the business sector, in the same way that white farmers still control most of the country's agricultural enterprises. Zimbabwe's relatively high per capita income should be seen in this context, for it disguises huge inequalities in wealth.

Socialist reforms

Rigid controls over the economy were necessary during the UDI years, as the country had to try to export and import goods secretly. When Robert Mugabe's government took over at Independence, it retained and indeed increased controls, in line with its Marxist-Leninist rhetoric about the need to 'seize the commanding heights of the economy'. To try to satisfy the people's high expectations, the government set about creating new jobs. This was reasonably easy in the political domain, in the civil service, and in the armed forces. New jobs were also created by the expansion of social services, such as health and education, and by the first wave of post-Independence foreign investment.

The government tried to protect workers by introducing minimum industrial, agricultural, and domestic wages, and by making it far more difficult for employers to sack workers. Price and wage controls operated side by side, in an attempt to protect the poor. These were well-intentioned and probably necessary responses to the colonial and exploitative economy which the government inherited, which had totally favoured employers. But (and the lessons for a free South Africa are clear) the impact did not always achieve the desired effect. On the land, many white farmers responded by reducing their workforce, by replacing workers with machines, and by converting full-time workers, who were fully protected by law, into nominally part-time workers, who were not. There has also been much evasion of minimum wage levels by blacks who hire people who are nominally 'family' members as domestic

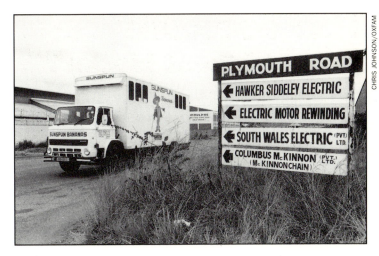

labour. In general, the regulations have served to deter employers from taking on more workers, rather than encouraging them to expand their workforces.

Some economists believe that Zimbabwe has the capacity to become a newly-industrialising country (a NIC) along the lines of South Korea or Singapore, provided that it can protect its own emerging industries, such as iron and steel, coal and manufacturing, by trade barriers. It is unlikely that the International Monetary Fund or the World Bank will allow Zimbabwe to develop in this way, since their policy always favours removing trade barriers, even though no country has ever succeeded in industrialising itself without medium-term protection for its products.

Southerton Industrial Estate, Harare

Post-Independence housing in Kambuzuma Township, Harare

Back on the capitalist road

By the late 1980s the economy was clearly not expanding anywhere near fast enough to be able to offer employment to the large number of new school leavers. There was much debate within the government over whether Zimbabwe should try to pursue a broadly socialist route or a capitalist path to development. Events elsewhere in Africa and in eastern Europe tended to support 'capitalist roaders' who, led by Bernard Chidzero, the Minister of Finance since Independence, are now in the ascendance. So Zimbabwe has made strong attempts to attract foreign investment. In 1989 there was an important conference in London involving the Confederation of British Industry (CBI) and its Zimbabwean counterpart, the CZI, at which Zimbabwe agreed to a new, more liberal, investment code and various other reforms. To some Zimbabweans present, it seemed as though the country was being sold to the highest bidder.

Structural adjustment: the impact on the poor

Zimbabwe's debt problem is nowhere near so severe as that of Zambia or Tanzania, and the economy is generally in a much stronger state than these countries. Nevertheless, the need for loans and investment has obliged the government to adopt an economic structural adjustment programme (known as ESAP), like most countries in Africa.

The adjustment programme, which began in 1991, entails the abolition of controls over prices and wages. In some contexts this may work well. In Zimbabwe it is already hitting the urban poor very hard, since prices have risen sharply following the removal of controls. Trade barriers and protection for local industry are being removed. The programme means that 10,000 civil servants and perhaps 20,000 workers in the private sector will lose their jobs. There are plans to reintroduce payments for health services, and, since January 1992, urban primary schools have been charging a

---

Promises, promises

'Proponents of structural adjustment and trade liberalisation tell us that this is what Zimbabwe should have done 11 years ago. We are told that the past 11 years saw experimentation with socialist policies go awry. We are told that with market forces allowed free play, things will, after an initial period of hardship, turn better. Attempts are made daily to persuade us that our bread will cost more, but we should take heart because it will be whiter.

All these promises and projections might well be correct. However, I do not know whether any of us will be favoured with good health to live long enough to witness any of this. We have memories of what it was like in the past. Our people witnessed 90 years of oppression in order to allow capital and free market forces to hold sway. There was unemployment – there still is. There was hunger, starvation and deprivation, and there still is.

We are talking about programmes and strategies that have an impact on the lives of people – real people. Time for them is exceedingly crucial. They want to see their lives improve now. After all, poverty is not a condition one tolerates like one's rowdy neighbour. Poverty means lack of freedom of choice, it means lack of access to power, it means inability to make plans for the future. Poverty is hopelessness.

How should the community of non-governmental organisations respond to structural adjustment and trade liberalisation? By buying more coffins and bandages, or by teaching mothers the art of feeding their babies less and less? Our business is to help people thrive and not just survive. Thriving is not measured in material things only, though that counts and is important in its own right. However, we are looking at the totality of the person, their dignity, their role in the decision-making processes that affect their lives, their freedom, and of course their security.'

(Paul Themba Nyathi, Director, Zimbabwe Project, July 1991)

minimum of Z$60 (£6.60) a year for children of parents earning less than Z$400 (£44.40) a month, while secondary school fees have been increased by 150 per cent. In rural areas, primary education remains free, and secondary school fees remain at Z$150 (£16.60) a year.

The government has set aside Z$20 million 'to shield disadvantaged or vulnerable groups' from the impact of these changes, but the effect of the programme has been immediate and painful. The value of the currency dropped by 50 per cent between August and November 1991, which (at one stroke) reduced the average annual income from more than £343 to about £200; on top of this, inflation rose to 30 per cent. Despite the government's provision, it is the poor and the vulnerable who will bear the brunt of this economic programme, which may well jeopardise the social gains achieved since Independence.

ESAP and the drought

The policies of the IMF and the World Bank have affected food security in Zimbabwe. Huge grain-storage silos, established by the Grain Marketing Board, are a familiar sight in the Zimbabwean landscape. For decades it has been government policy to try to store the equivalent of one year's maize production, as a precaution against drought. This strategy has served Zimbabwe and its neighbours well. (In recent years, for example, donor nations supplying emergency food aid to Mozambique have bought Zimbabwean maize and paid for it to be sent by rail to Beira and Maputo, rather than shipping food from overseas.)

However, in 1990-91 the IMF and the World Bank put heavy pressure on the Zimbabwean government to sell off its 'uneconomic' state-run institutions, or to reduce investment in them. Consequently, the Grain Marketing Board was obliged to sell off its huge stockpile of maize, and to stop building grain silos in outlying areas. As a result, one year later, Zimbabwe found itself having to import, at enormous cost, the equivalent of what it had recently stockpiled: nearly two million tonnes.

For many Zimbabweans, there is an unpalatable irony in the fact that subsidies for farmers in the USA and Europe are acceptable to the IMF and World Bank, but similar subsidies are apparently inappropriate for farmers in Zimbabwe and elsewhere in Africa.

GREG WILLIAMS/SELECT

May 1992: Dzingai Madhoro on his farm at Mandamabgwe, Chivi District: one of thousands of farmers ruined by the drought

City life

VISITORS TO HARARE, Zimbabwe's capital, are often surprised to see a modern, bustling, American-style city with familiar names like Barclays Bank, Woolworths, and Wimpy. Depending on their preconceptions, they feel either pleasantly surprised or disappointed that Harare is not 'more African'.

The towns and cities of Rhodesia were segregated. There were white suburbs and black suburbs. In Salisbury (now Harare) most whites lived north of the railway line, most blacks south of it. There were class divisions too, which tended to be more marked among whites than blacks, who were seen as an undifferentiated mass by the settlers. Blacks who lived in white suburbs did so only as domestic servants. Typically, they lived in shacks at the bottom of the master's garden. Visitors who created 'noise' were not welcomed. The spacious northern suburbs grew in opulence after 1945. A visitor flying into Harare today is struck by the number of swimming pools: the scene from the air looks more like California than Africa.

Street scene in downtown Harare

The city centres were owned and controlled exclusively by white people. Black workers were of course needed to work in industry, serve in shops, act as messengers, sell ice creams, and clean the streets. At night they all disappeared, as though by magic, back to the black suburbs. They had to carry passes which strictly limited their movements.

All of this has changed radically and visibly since Independence. Whereas Salisbury was clearly a white city, Harare is now definitely a black city. Whites still live there, but they no longer dominate the scene. Black Zimbabweans no longer have to wait for white citizens to be served first in shops. City centres are no longer deserted at night, as they once were. Local black musicians have replaced the imported music of Jim Reeves, Cliff Richard, and Roger Whittaker in popular esteem.

The expansion of the cities

Since 1980, there has been a rush to the cities in search of jobs and a better standard of living. Nobody knows for certain, but the urban growth rate has probably been around 10 per cent a year since 1980. After Independence sanctions were lifted, investment arrived, and many new jobs were created, especially in the civil service. There was a major housing programme in all the main towns. Transport networks were expanded. Price controls were retained, to the benefit of all. Small, informal businesses mushroomed. For the first time, blacks were allowed to sell vegetables, fruits and handicrafts in the city centres and in the former white suburbs – now referred to euphemistically as 'low-density' suburbs. (The former black suburbs are now 'high-density'.)

CHRIS JOHNSON/OXFAM

Privileges for the new élite

Racial segregation has been replaced by class segregation, although in many respects these new social divisions are less clear cut, and the issues more confused. At one extreme, the black professional classes and 'chefs' (the new political élite) have moved into the once exclusively white suburbs, where distances make car ownership essential. Cynics believed that once a former freedom fighter, newly-turned government minister, moved into a large house with a swimming pool in the suburb of Mount Pleasant, his enthusiasm for social transformation might become blunted.

On the whole, the cynics have been proved right. There is now a highly visible and wealthy black upper-middle class, which shares many of the attitudes of its white predecessors. Robert Mugabe's attempts to impose an effective Leadership Code, to limit the acquisition of wealth and business interests by leading politicians, have clearly failed. There is extensive corruption in high political circles, as was revealed in the notorious 'Willowgate' scandal of 1988, which involved the illegal importation and sale of motor cars for huge profits by senior political figures. The subsequent public inquiry revealed the depth of popular contempt for the ruling chefs.

Problems for the middle classes

For the black middle-classes, some of whom have moved into the northern suburbs, independence has brought new opportunities, new aspirations – and new frustrations. During the second half of the 1980s, life became increasingly difficult. The effects of inflation started to bite, and the cost of living rose steadily – but more rapidly for the poor than for the rich. After the initial boom, very few jobs were created. The forecast from 1991 was that something like 300,000 young people will leave school each year, to compete for scarce jobs.

Investment in public transport has been low. The state of city buses in Harare is appalling. People are forced to leave home hours before they start work, in order to fight their way on to the inadequate number of buses going into town. Then they have to repeat the process in the evening. Long-distance buses are often involved in fatal accidents following tyre blow-outs. Official explanations talk of lack of foreign exchange for tyres or spare parts. Yet 'forex' always seems to be available when prestigious events are being held, such as the Commonwealth Heads of Government Conference in Harare in October 1991. It is essentially a question of priority.

BRIAN BEARDWOOD/OXFAM

Remoulding tyres in Bulawayo: lack of raw materials and foreign exchange means a chronic shortage of vehicle parts

A nightmare for the urban poor

The plight of the urban poor, for whom there is almost no state welfare provision, may well get worse under trade liberalisation and structural adjustment. Already most price controls have been removed, so there is no longer any cushion for the poor. They will also have to pay for both health and education. There is no one to defend their interests. The already large number of beggars on the streets is likely to increase. Harare is now home to an army of destitute and homeless people, largely forgotten by the authorities, and forced to rely on begging and occasional charitable handouts.

CHRIS JOHNSON/OXFAM

Unseen and unseeing: a destitute man begging in Harare

Down and out in 'Sunshine City'

The homeless of Harare are the 'Twilight People'. They appear on the streets at dusk, lurking in shop doorways and grubbing about in refuse bins for food and anything else that may be useful in their daily struggle to survive. Evicted from their makeshift shanty towns by the authorities, their prospects are bleak. They can only look forward to further harassment and a grim battle to keep body and soul together. But they won't go away; they can't. They simply have nowhere to go.

During the day, it's business as usual in the commercial sector of town. The pavements are clear; only the odd tell-tale bundle of rags or collection of cardboard is visible. It is the squatters' bedding, but they are nowhere to be seen. Only after 5 pm, when the shops have closed, do dozens of dirty, roughly dressed individuals gradually appear, loitering around or sitting on window sills. By 9 pm they are already asleep, wrapped in tattered blankets, cardboard boxes, or plastic sheets. In the doorway of Adams Brothers' clothes shop lives Collin Zimuto, who tells this story:

'I was born in Gwanda District. My parents died before I could complete my secondary education.

Relatives were unwilling to help, so I moved into Harare in search of a job, but of course there's nothing.'

Asked what sort of people sleep on the pavement together with him, he says: 'We even have graduates here. Form Sixes and Fours are numerous among us. Some are even employed and have no accommodation. But these are only a few. Most of these' (he waves a hand at the line of sleepers) 'are jobless, the cripples, the mentally retarded, the blind, and all sorts. Come at 11 pm and see for yourself, the whole pavement will be fully occupied.'

Collin goes on to describe how they live in fear. They have experienced numerous raids by the Municipal Police, who come in trucks. Then, he says, the squatters have to run for their lives. He has bitter memories of how they were handled at Chikurubi when they were evicted from Eastlea. 'We were beaten, and the food was not sufficient.' He is quiet for a moment, then adds, 'Those shining boots are dreadful.'

Such is the fate of the homeless in the 'Sunshine Capital'!
(Julius Zava, *Parade*, February 1991)

Disillusionment sets in

People compare their plight with the lives of the rich 'chefs'. Because the daily newspapers have been muzzled, it is in the monthlies such as *Parade* and *Moto*, which people eagerly buy on street corners, that they voice their grievances – about the lack of jobs, the increasing cost of living, and the lifestyles of the rich. Particularly bitter are the ex-combatants who fought in the war of liberation, many of whom are now unemployed. Heroes in their time, they are now largely forgotten. ('Everybody asks: "Do you have five O-levels?" Where do they expect an unemployed ex-combatant to get such a qualification?' demands a recent correspondent in *Parade*.)

Disillusionment has certainly increased among an urban population which is highly politicised. This was revealed in the 1990 election by massive abstentions and by a large vote for the opposition ZUM party led by Edgar Tekere – even though ZUM had almost nothing to offer them, and had been seriously compromised by its alliance with Ian Smith and his colleagues.

There are real dangers that the hard-won gains of the first decade of independence may be lost in the 1990s.

JERRY HARDMAN-JONES

Melancholy Girl, 1988, by Tapfuma Gutsa

The rich get richer

'Don't mean to sound bitter – yes, I do mean to sound bitter, but it seems to me for all the ideals our independence is supposed to represent, it's still the same old ox-wagon of the rich getting richer and the poor getting poorer. There's even an attempt to make poverty a holy and acceptable condition. You say you're hungry, and the chef peers over his three chins down at you and says "Comrade, you're the backbone of the revolution" – as if your life's ambition is to be as thin and lean as a mosquito's backbone. And you try to say "Chef, I don't want to be the backbone, I want to be the big belly of the struggle against neo-colonialism like the one you got there underneath that Castro beard". And before you even finish what you're saying he's got the CIO [Central Intelligence Organisation] and the police and you are being marched at gunpoint to the interrogation barracks.'

(Dambudzo Marachera: *Mindblast, or The Definitive Buddy.* [9])

Culture
– ancient and modern

ON 21 JULY 1990 in the Yorkshire Sculpture Park near Wakefield in England, Joshua Nkomo, the Vice President of Zimbabwe, opened an exhibition of Zimbabwean stone sculpture, organised to coincide with Zimbabwe's tenth anniversary celebrations. For four months the English countryside provided the backdrop to the largest ever open-air exhibition of contemporary African stone carving; over 300,000 people went to see it. In similar fashion, British clubs and recording studios have welcomed Zimbabwean bands and musicians, such as Thomas Mapfumo and the Bhundu Boys, since the mid-1980s. Some are now established and respected players on the international musical scene.

PETER MCCULLOCH/OXFAM

Maxwell Gochera, an award-winning student of carving at the National Gallery School

Cream teas and Coca-Cola

For many years, however, the traffic had moved in the opposite direction, as Rhodesia's settler society surrounded itself with cultural reminders of home. Cream teas are still served in Zimbabwe's botanical gardens; the department stores that line the boulevards of its city centres look like a scene from the Home Counties in the 1950s; the robed choir in Harare's Anglican cathedral is reminiscent of any English cathedral close, except that it sings with an uninhibited vitality rarely found in its more reserved country of origin.

After the British came the 'Coca-Cola culture': Harare boasts the latest Hollywood movies and fashions in international cuisine; children grow up on imported American TV soaps, and shun their native 'sadza' for burgers and chips; chart-topping British pop songs belt out from city-centre boutiques and bars; the lifts and lounges of the high-class hotels succumb to muzak's torpor. But beneath this veneer of cosmopolitan sophistication, a wealth of indigenous cultural activity thrives, as the abstract carvings on the Yorkshire hillside bear witness.

Rocks and stones

The earliest surviving examples of traditional art are probably the ancient rock paintings which can still be seen in caves and on granite hillsides throughout Zimbabwe. Most were painted at least 2,500 years ago, and depict scenes from daily life – hunting, dancing, and feasting. These two-dimensional people and their animals provide clues to the everyday activities of their makers, but the paintings also hint at deeper spiritual values and beliefs. Traditional religion provides the inspiration and the impetus for many Zimbabwean art forms, both ancient (as in the rock paintings) and modern (as in Shona stone sculpture).

Zimbabwe's stone ruins are evidence of former architectural skills. The most impressive of these, Great Zimbabwe, is thought to have been built around 1250 AD, and was the most powerful Shona capital of its age. Up on the Acropolis, where most of the soapstone 'Zimbabwe birds' were discovered, one can look down across the valley to the Great Enclosure, with its vast perimeter dry-stone wall surrounding a maze of corridors and chambers, above which looms the famous Conical Tower. Ten minutes' walk from this imposing yet tranquil site lies a modern hotel, complete with souvenir shop and comfortable chalets – an illustration of contemporary Zimbabwe's confusing cultural identity.

Politics and culture: music and poetry in modern Zimbabwe

Political struggle has been another powerful cultural force, both before and after Independence. During the war of liberation, from its base in Mozambique, ZANU broadcast news, messages, and encouragement to its supporters back home. One popular programme was 'Chimurenga Requests' – songs of protest banned by the Smith regime. The singer Thomas Mapfumo, who was placed in detention by the authorities, recalls:

> I started out as a rock 'n roll singer, doing some of Presley's numbers, Little Richard – and soul. Especially Otis Redding. To be frank, I had no direction. Then I realised no, the people of Zimbabwe, we are lost, we are following the wrong track. We are supposed to do our own music. That gave me the courage to compose my own songs in Shona.
>
> The situation was changing at that time, and there was a lot of political unrest in this country. We were starting to fight for our freedom. ... Then even the music started changing, and I thought I could do my country a

favour – to sing 'Chimurenga' songs, so as to encourage those boys who were fighting in the bush. I knew then that I must use my own African language to send a message to my own people.[10]

Political independence has not silenced Mapfumo's voice, nor tempered his language. Along with other artists and writers, students and intellectuals, he has continued to use his talents to speak out against corruption, censorship, and political betrayal.

The poems of Freedom Nyamubaya, a young woman who fought with the liberation army during the war, capture the pain and the brutality of armed conflict, but they also suggest that the struggle is far from won, and that the vision of those who fought for social change and justice has been betrayed by new leaders.

Thomas Mapfumo at a World Music concert in England, 1990

MARIAN POCOCK

A Mysterious Marriage

Once upon a time
there was a boy and girl
forced to leave their home
by armed robbers.
The boy was Independence
The girl was Freedom.
While fighting back, they got married.

After the big war they went back home.
Everybody prepared for the wedding.
Drinks and food abounded,
Even the disabled felt able.
The whole village gathered waiting.
Freedom and Independence
were more popular than Jesus.

Independence came
But Freedom was not there.
An old woman saw Freedom's shadow passing,
Walking through the crowd, Freedom to the gate.
All the same, they celebrated for Independence.

Independence is now a senior bachelor.
Some people still talk about him
Many others take no notice.
A lot still say it was a fake marriage.
You can't be a husband without a wife.
Fruitless and barren Independence staggers to old age,
Since her shadow, Freedom, hasn't come.

Freedom Nyamubaya [11]

Arts in the community

Community-based groups also draw on the special powers of art to move and inform. They use music, role-plays and dance to increase awareness and understanding of social issues. The 'Tose Sonke' Disabled Theatre Company, formed in 1985, is a practical example of integration in action. Its disabled and non-disabled members use theatre to challenge negative assumptions about disability, and to demonstrate the positive contribution that both groups can make to society when living and working alongside each other. One of the group's actors describes their work:

Many come to see our shows out of a sense of pity, it seems. For them it is just another way of donating to people with disabilities. However, after a show it is not unusual for members of the audience to come up and talk to us. They tell us that they would never have thought that they could learn from a person with a disability.

We listen to parents and advise them to go to their nearest rehabilitation department if it is appropriate. By doing this we, too, are trying to encourage communities to look after their own people with the help of rehabilitation workers, and not to rush them straight off to an institution. [12]

BRIAN BEARDWOOD/OXFAM

Duba Duba, an Ndebele a cappella choir, sings at parties and in beer halls on Sunday nights in Mabutweni Township

GAVIN FILM LTD.

A scene from *Jit*: our hero is confronted by his guiding spirit, the Jukwa. She urges the hustler to return home to his village – and demands a bigger libation of beer!

Jit is a hit

At the 1990 London Film Festival an up-beat entertaining movie called *Jit* received a standing ovation. It was the first film to be made in Zimbabwe with local financial backing, a sign that cinema is beginning to be seen as more than a form of imported entertainment. With local actors, local technicians, and a soundtrack filled with more than a dozen of Zimbabwe's top bands and musicians, the low-budget *Jit* displayed the country's talent, rather than just the beauty of its scenery, which until then had been the main attraction for international film-makers.

An enduring culture?

The quality of Zimbabwean art forms – literature, poetry, sculpture, and music – is now widely recognised. Equally impressive is the sheer range of cultural experiences which Zimbabwe has to offer – from the legends of oral history to international book fairs; solidarity rock concerts in Harare's stadium, and songs sung by village women in health education gatherings; small road-side craft-stalls and elegant urban art galleries; a firm belief in the powers of traditional healers and leaders, alongside a commitment to the principles of a modern democratic state.

In the years since Independence, African artists and intellectuals have striven to create the outlets for their talents which had been denied them during the colonial period. However, they continue to struggle for political space and have not yet established their right to dissent, despite a burst of flamboyant non-conformism from the writer Dambudzo Marachera (*'Will the poem sing flatteries Or smell out the rot in public places?'*). At the same time, travel and technology make the world seem smaller, with cultures merging in one international melting-pot. Time will tell whether Zimbabwe's artists and thinkers manage to resist these pressures, or whether external influences will eventually swamp Zimbabwe's re-emerging national culture.

JERRY HARDMAN-JONES

Chapungu, 1985, by Bernard Matemera (a former cattle herder and early member of the Tengengene Sculpture Community)

53

Sport:
a national obsession

ZIMBABWEANS have always been fanatical about sport. Large crowds attend major events, eager to watch football, horse racing, athletics, rugby, hockey, and cricket matches. President Mugabe, a keen cricket fan, attends matches against visiting international sides whenever he can. A perfect climate encourages sportsmen and women of all ages to develop their skills.

In the colonial past, white Rhodesian teams competed against South African provincial sides in domestic competitions. It was not unusual for Rhodesians to win Springbok caps in cricket, rugby and hockey. After Independence, Zimbabwean sport severed its links with South Africa and became non-racial, and the country has entered the international arena. It has competed in Olympic Games, winning the Gold Medal for hockey in Moscow 1980, while its cricket and rugby teams have qualified for World Cup competitions – its cricketers beating Australia in 1983, and England in 1992. (*England roasted by Zimbabwe paceman* reported the *Daily Mail* on 19 March, adding the laconic comment of chicken farmer and fast bowler Eddo Brandes: 'I just run up and bowl'.)

Two of Zimbabwe's finest sportsmen, the footballer Bruce Grobbelaar and the cricketer Graeme Hick, have become internationally famous.

Graeme Hick: 15,000 not out

Graeme Hick learned his sporting skills as a child after Zimbabwe's independence. He broke most of the schoolboy batting records at Prince Edward School, Harare, and then went to play in England for Worcestershire in 1984 at the age of 18. He has since developed into one of the world's greatest batsmen, hitting the ball with awesome power. Because Zimbabwe has not yet been given full Test Match status, Hick set his heart on playing for England. Unable to produce a convincing British parent or grandparent, he has been obliged to serve an exceptionally long qualifying period. This ended in the summer of 1991, when Hick made his debut for England against the West Indies at the age of 24.

In his brief career, Hick has already broken many batting records. In 1988 he made a stunning 405 not out against Somerset, the second highest score ever

Graeme Hick in action for Worcestershire County Cricket Club

WORCESTER EVENING NEWS

made in England. In 1990 he reached 50 first-class centuries at a younger age than anyone in the history of the game, breaking Don Bradman's previous record. He has now scored over 15,000 first-class runs. Time will tell if this young Zimbabwean continues to rewrite the record books.

Bruce Grobbelaar: a Zimbabwean in Liverpool

Bruce Grobbelaar has been Liverpool's first-choice goalkeeper since joining the club from Vancouver Whitecaps in 1981 at the age of 23 for a fee of £250,000. He proceeded to play an amazing 317 consecutive matches for Britain's most successful club, before injury forced him out for a few games in 1986. Known variously as 'Jungle Man' or 'Clown', Grobbelaar is both a brilliant goalkeeper and a character who loves to entertain crowds. At the end of one cup final, he walked the length of the Wembley pitch on his hands to win a bet. In the decisive penalty shoot-out at the 1984 European Cup Final, he performed a 'Jungle Man' dance routine which successfully intimidated the Roma penalty kickers and won the match for Liverpool.

Grobbelaar fought, came under fire, and killed while serving as a conscript in the Rhodesian army during the war of Independence in 1975-77. The experience left deep scars. He still dreams about its horrors. His autobiography is dedicated 'To all my friends who died in a needless war'. He admits that travel and maturity have helped him to outgrow the racist attitudes he was brought up with. He has played World Cup qualifying matches for Zimbabwe in the past, and has reapplied for a Zimbabwean passport in the hope of playing for his native country again: 'Zimbabwe, for all my travels, is my home and always will be', he affirms in his autobiography. Grobbelaar is optimistic that Zimbabwe 'will prosper and become one of the outstanding African nations'.[13]

LIVERPOOL DAILY POST AND ECHO

Bruce Grobbelaar in goal for Liverpool City

Conclusion:
a land divided?

VISITORS who travel beyond the city centres and tourist resorts cannot fail to be struck by the contrasts in Zimbabwean society. It accommodates urban sophistication, high-tech agriculture, and the bureaucratic trappings of a modern state alongside street beggars, peasant farming, and the richness of its traditional culture. There are shocking disparities of wealth and resources, and – as in most developing countries – even Nature casts an uneven shadow over rich and poor.

Some of these divisions are inherited, the legacy of colonial oppression and exploitation. Others have been exacerbated by external pressures: a decade of South African destabilisation; an economy now tied to the interests of world markets and international capital; an urban culture seduced by the superficiality of Western consumerism.

Other divisions, though, have little to do with race, colour, or political creed. Nor can they be explained away as the result of Zimbabwe's geographical and economic vulnerability. They have everything to do with money, power, social class, and the age-old gulf between those who have and those who have not.

But a picture of a divided and troubled Zimbabwe would be incomplete. This book has also shown the achievements of a newly-independent country in the provision of health care and education for all its people, in its art, music, and literature, in the growth of indigenous business and commerce, and in the nation's collective commitment to racial reconciliation and mutual understanding.

This book has sought to introduce some of the individuals and organisations who are actively seeking ways of bridging divisions and building better lives for themselves, their families, and communities. In small ways, right across Zimbabwe, there are people dedicated to achieving that goal – a mother engaged in a cottage industry to earn the extra cash needed for her children's school fees; a farmer passing on to his community his hard-won skills in water conservation; a disabled actor using his talents to challenge prejudice and foster understanding.

The challenge for Zimbabwe is to find ways of fulfilling these aspirations and of replicating at a corporate and national level the values and the spirit which lie behind them. The challenge is also to accept that *diversity* does not equal *division*: to accept that people have the right to a voice in their own develop-ment and future, and to respect that right, even if it brings with it diverse views of what that future might be.

Zimbabwe today hangs in the balance. The honeymoon years of Independence have long since gone. Disillusion has crept in as the economy weakens and the country faces the disaster of drought. The potential for political and social crisis is clearly present. And yet Zimbabweans have shown in the past their capacity to persevere and to succeed against the odds. The support of the international community will be needed in the struggle. But in its people Zimbabwe has demonstrated that it has the spirit and the strength to tip the scales in the direction of tolerance, peace, and development for the good of all. Those who know and love Zimbabwe will wish it well in that endeavour.

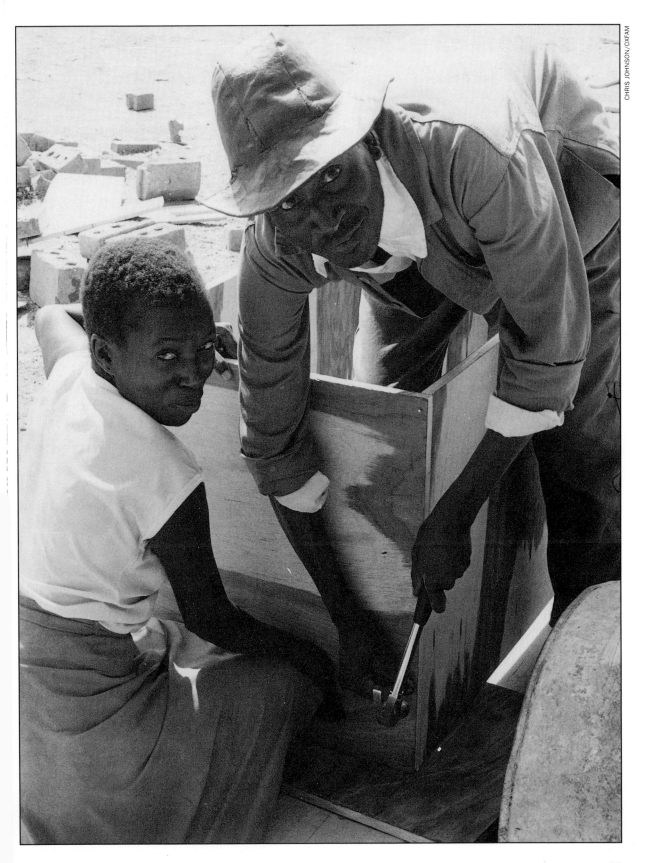

A chronology of a nation

1000 Shona people began settling in Zimbabwe.

c.1250 Great Zimbabwe state, a flourishing trading empire.

1450 Followed by Mutapa (c.1450-1700), Torwa (c.1450-1650), and Rozvi (c.1690-1840) states.

1510 First Portuguese traders arrived.

1840 Ndebele people, originally from South Africa, settled in west of Zimbabwe around Bulawayo.

1859 First Christian missionary station established among Ndebele.

1886 Discovery of gold around Johannesburg led to scramble for Southern Africa.

1889 Cecil Rhodes received Royal Charter from British Government for his British South Africa Company (to exploit gold and other minerals), and given powers of government.

1890 BSA Company and white settlers invaded and occupied Mashonaland (northern and eastern part of country). British flag raised at Salisbury (now Harare).

1893 Whites conquered Matabeleland (western Zimbabwe). Country became known as Southern Rhodesia, later Rhodesia.

1896-7 Shona and Ndebele rose up in attempt to throw off white rule. Known as *First Chimurenga* (War of Liberation). Thousands killed.

1923 BSA Company gave up administration. White settlers took charge. Southern Rhodesia became 'self-governing colony'.

1930 Land Apportionment Act. Basic discriminatory land law.

1934 Industrial Conciliation Act. Basic discriminatory labour law.

1953 Southern Rhodesia joined Northern Rhodesia (Zambia) and Nyasaland (Malawi) in Federation of Rhodesia and Nyasaland, created by Britain despite much black opposition. Dissolved in 1963.

1957 Formation of Southern Rhodesia African National Congress, first modern black nationalist party, led by Joshua Nkomo. After being banned, in 1961 it became ZAPU (Zimbabwe African People's Union).

1963 Formation of ZANU (Zimbabwe African National Union), as rival political party to ZAPU.

1965 Unilateral Declaration of Independence by Prime Minister Ian Smith and white settlers in an attempt to ward off African majority rule.

1966 *Second Chimurenga* (War of Liberation) began. Helped by guerrilla bases established in Mozambique and Zambia. Estimated 27,500 people died by 1980.

1974 Military coup in Portugal led to the overthrow of Portuguese colonial empire and independence of Mozambique in 1975, allowing extensive guerrilla infiltration into Rhodesia across eastern border.

1979 Lancaster House Constitution hammered out in London to end war and prepare for independence.

1980 First free election won by Robert Mugabe's ZANU (PF) party. Country became independent as Zimbabwe, 18 April.

1982-7 Intermittent war in Matabeleland waged by dissidents. Thousands of civilians killed.

1987 Unity accord between ZANU and Joshua Nkomo's ZAPU brought an end to war. Mugabe became first executive president.

1989 ZANU and ZAPU merged parties.

1990 Tenth anniversary of Independence. Lancaster House Constitution amended. Expected introduction of one-party state abandoned.

Introduction of Economic Structural Adjustment Programme (ESAP)

1991 Zimbabwe hosted Commonwealth Heads of Government meeting.

1992 Passing of the Land Acquisition Act.

Sources and further reading

Village primary school, Insuza Resettlement Area

Andre Astrow, *Zimbabwe: A Revolution That Lost Its Way?* (London: Zed Books, 1983).

David Caute, *Under the Skin: The Death of White Rhodesia* (London: Penguin, 1983).

Julie Frederikse, *None But Ourselves: Masses vs. Media in the Making of Zimbabwe* (London: James Currey, 1982).

Bruce Grobbelaar with Bob Harris, *Bring on the Clown* (London: Collins, 1988).

Bruce Grobbelaar with Bob Harris, *Bruce Grobbelaar: An Autobiography* (London: Coronet, 1988).

Jeffrey Herbst, *State Politics in Zimbabwe* (Berkeley and Los Angeles: University of California Press, 1990).

Graeme Hick, *My Early Life* (London: Macmillan, 1991).

David Lan, *Guns and Rain: Guerrillas and Spirit Mediums in Zimbabwe* (London: James Currey, 1985).

Mary McAllister, Helen House and Cathy Naidoo, *Zimbabwe Steps Ahead: Community Rehabilitation and People with Disabilities* (London: Catholic Institute for International Relations, 1990).

Barbara McCrea and Tony Pinchuck, *Zimbabwe and Botswana: The Rough Guide* (Bromley: Harrap-Columbus, 1990).

Ibbo Mandaza (ed), *Zimbabwe: The Political Economy of Transition, 1980-1986* (Dakar: CODESRIA, 1986).

David Martin and Phyllis Johnson, *The Struggle for Zimbabwe* (London: Faber, 1981).

Robin Palmer, *Land and Racial Domination in Rhodesia* (Berkeley and Los Angeles: University of California Press, 1977).

Ian Phimister, *An Economic and Social History of Zimbabwe, 1890-1948: Capital Accumulation and Class Struggle* (Harlow: Longman, 1988).

Terence Ranger, *Peasant Consciousness and Guerrilla War in Zimbabwe* (London: James Currey, 1985).

Irene Staunton (ed), *Mothers of the Revolution: The War Experiences of Thirty Zimbabwean Women* (London: James Currey, 1991).

Colin Stoneman and Lionel Cliffe, *Zimbabwe: Politics, Economics and Society* (London: Pinter, 1989).

Colin Stoneman (ed), *Zimbabwe's Prospects* (London: Macmillan, 1988).

Colin Stoneman (ed), *Zimbabwe's Inheritance* (London: Macmillan, 1981).

Zimbabwe: A Break with the Past? Human Rights and Political Unity (New York, Washington, London: Africa Watch Report, 1989).

Books published in Zimbabwe

Diana Auret, *A Decade of Development: Zimbabwe 1980-1990* (Gweru: Mambo Press, 1990).

Canaan S. Banana (ed), *Turmoil and Tenacity: Zimbabwe 1890-1990* (Harare: The College Press, 1989).

Denis Berens (ed), *A Concise Encyclopedia of Zimbabwe* (Gweru: Mambo Press, 1988).

Martin de Graaf and Brigid Willmore, *The Importance of People* (Bulawayo: Hlekweni FRSC, 1987).

John Iliffe, *Famine in Zimbabwe 1890-1960* (Gweru: Mambo Press, 1990).

Helen Jackson, *AIDS: Action Now: Information, Prevention and Support in Zimbabwe* (Harare: AIDS Counselling Trust, 1988).

Khuluma Usenza, *The Story of the Organisation of Rural Associations for Progress in Zimbabwe's Rural Development* (Bulawayo: ORAP, 1985).

Bruce Moore-King, *White Man Black War* (Harare: Baobab Books, 1988).

Ibbo Mandaza and Lloyd Sachikonye (eds), *The One-Party State and Democracy: the Zimbabwe Debate* (Harare: SAPES Trust, 1991).

Andrew Nyathi with John Hoffman, *Tomorrow is Built Today* (Harare: Anvil Press, 1990).

Peter Roussos, *Zimbabwe: An Introduction to the Economics of Transformation* (Harare: Baobab Books, 1988).

Zimbabwe Epic (Harare: National Archives of Zimbabwe, 1984).

Zimbabwe Women's Bureau, *We Carry a Heavy Load* (Harare: Zimbabwe Women's Bureau, 1981).

Magazines published in Zimbabwe

Africa South

Horizon

Moto

Parade

Social Change and Development

Southern African Economist

Southern African Review of Books

Southern Africa Political and Economic Monthly

Zimbabwe Bird (1990) by Agnes Nyanhongo, a former shop assistant who began sculpting in 1987

JERRY HARDMAN-JONES

Books on southern Africa

Samir Amin, Derrick Chitala and Ibbo Mandaza (eds), *SADCC: Prospects for Disengagement and Development in Southern Africa* (London: United Nations University and Zed Books, 1987).

Victoria Brittain, *Hidden Lives, Hidden Deaths: South Africa's Crippling of a Continent* (London: Faber, 1988).

Donald Denoon and Balam Nyeko, *Southern Africa since 1800* (Harlow: Longman, 1984).

Joseph Hanlon, *Apartheid's Second Front: South Africa's War Against Its Neighbours* (London: Penguin, 1986).

Joseph Hanlon, *Beggar Your Neighbours: Apartheid Power in Southern Africa* (London: James Currey, 1986).

Joseph Hanlon/Economist Intelligence Unit, *SADCC in the 1990s* (London: EIU, 1989).

Phyllis Johnson and David Martin, *Apartheid Terrorism: The Destabilization Report* (London: Commonwealth Secretariat and James Currey, 1989).

Phyllis Johnson and David Martin (eds), *Destructive Engagement: Southern Africa at War* (Harare: Zimbabwe Publishing House, 1986).

Preben Kaarsholm (ed), *Cultural Struggle and Development in Southern Africa* (London: James Currey, 1991).

William Minter, *King Solomon's Mines Revisited: Western Interests and the Burdened History of Southern Africa* (New York: Basic Books, 1986).

John Omer-Cooper, *History of Southern Africa* (London: James Currey, 1987).

Robin Palmer and Neil Parsons, *The Roots of Rural Poverty in Central and Southern Africa* (London: Heinemann Educational Books, 1977).

Neil Parsons, *A New History of Southern Africa* (London: Macmillan, 1983).

Susanna Smith, *Front Line Africa: The Right to a Future* (Oxford: Oxfam, 1990).

Carol Thompson, *Challenge to Imperialism: The Frontline States in the Liberation of Zimbabwe* (Harare: Zimbabwe Publishing House, 1985).

Leroy Vail (ed), *The Creation of Tribalism in Southern Africa* (London: James Currey, 1989).

Horse (1988) by Ephraim Chaurika, a former watch repairer and founder member of the Tengenenge Sculptors' Community

JERRY HARDMAN-JONES

Notes

1 Vere Stent: *A Personal Record of Some Incidents in the Life of Cecil Rhodes* (Cape Town: Maskew Miller, 1925, pp. 45-6).

2 Irene Staunton: *Mothers of the Revolution: The War Experiences of Thirty Zimbabwean Women* (Harare: Baobab/London: James Currey, 1991).

3 Bruce Grobbelaar with Bob Harris: *Bruce Grobbelaar: An Autobiography* (London: Coronet, 1988, pp. 187-8).

4 Lewis Hastings: *Dragons Are Extra* (London: Penguin, 1947, p. 129).

5 Thomas Morgan Thomas: *Eleven Years in Central South Africa* (London: John Snow, 1873).

6 Extract from an article by Andrew Meldrum, reprinted with permission from *Africa South*, March/April 1991.

7 Roy Henson, a founder and co-director of Hlekweni, writing in *The Importance of People*, a collection of essays published to mark the twentieth anniversary of Hlekweni's foundation.

8 Quoted in 'A new approach to the disabled in Africa' by Chris McIvor in *The Courier*, 124, November/December 1990.

9 Reproduced with permission from *Mindblast, or The Definitive Buddy* by Dambudzo Marachera (Harare: The College Press, 1984).

10 Thomas Mapfumo, quoted in *None But Ourselves: Masses vs. Media in the Making of Zimbabwe*, by Julie Frederikse (London: James Currey, 1982).

11 Reproduced with permission from *On the Road Again*, by Freedom Nyamubaya (Harare: Zimbabwe Publishing House, 1986).

12 Reproduced with permission from *Zimbabwe Steps Ahead: Community Rehabilitation and People with Disabilities* by Mary McAlister, Helen House, and Cathy Naidoo (London: Catholic Institute for International Relations, 1990).

13 Bruce Grobbelaar with Bob Harris: *Bruce Grobbelaar: An Autobiography* (London: Coronet, 1988).

14 *On the Road Again*, by Freedom Nyamubaya (Harare: Zimbabwe Publishing House, 1986).

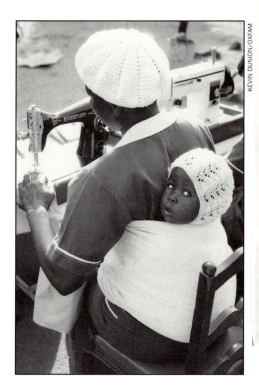

KEVIN DUNION/OXFAM

Acknowledgements

The authors are grateful for the help of the following people:

Peter Coleridge, Jerry Hardman-Jones, Richard Moseley-Williams, Peter Nyoni, Colin Stoneman, Richard Tallontire, James Tumwine, Ken Wilson

The Valley

Once again dawn turns to dusk,
Where life is at peace and minds at rest.
The orange sky spreads the last rays,
With the island-like clouds
Splitting into different shapes,
Clearing a passage for the half-sunk sun.
Dande: a village at work on its finishing touches.

The little boys chant war songs,
While they drive the cattle home.
With piles of wood on their shoulders,
Fathers rush home to catch up with the dying light.
The well-balanced clay pots and buckets
Head-rest on the single-filing mothers,
It's nothing but water, creatures' necessity.

Across Utete river lies Centenary,
A huge complex of commercial farming,
Where land remains green throughout the year
From over-flowing dams and boreholes.

The villagers were made for piece work.
At rain-request ceremony they gather around a pot of beer
Half-excited, half-depressed,
From the drought that left everybody starving.
But still life goes,
They feel at home.

Freedom Nyamubaya [14]

LIBA TAYLOR/PANOS

Oxfam in Zimbabwe

Most of the projects featured in this book are funded by Oxfam (UK and Ireland). Oxfam opened an office in Zimbabwe on the eve of the country's independence in 1980 (although before that some social welfare projects had been funded in Rhodesia, and among Zimbabwean refugees in Mozambique and Zambia).

In the immediate post-war years, the priority for Oxfam was rehabilitation and reconstruction work, especially in health and rural development. As the programme developed, it maintained its rural base, but began to focus on certain main areas: primary health care; training; community development; disability and development; and support (direct and indirect) for co-operatives.

In recent years Oxfam has sought ways of adapting to the needs created by Zimbabwe's rapidly-changing economic and social environment. In the year ending April 1992, a total of £419,406 was allocated to work in Zimbabwe. Of this, almost £100,000 went on drought-relief measures, and the rest was used to support the self-help enterprises of a wide range of organisations.

Ekuphumuleni ('a place of peace') is an Oxfam-funded nursing home for 42 old people in Bulawayo. Its home-based care programme also supports elderly people and their carers living in the community.

Oxfam, 274 Banbury Road, Oxford, OX2, England. Registered as a charity, no. 202918.